~The Gift of Words

There was a child went forth every day,
And the first object he looked upon and received with
    wonder or pity or love or dread, that object
    he became,
And that object became part of him for the day or a certain
    part of the day. . . or for many years or stretching
    cycles of years. . .

                      —Walt Whitman

~The Gift of Words

WRITING AND LITERATURE
IN THE ELEMENTARY CLASSROOM

PAULA ROOD AND LUCREZIA IACOMINO

Addison-Wesley Publishing Company

Menlo Park, California ~ Reading, Massachusetts ~ New York
Don Mills, Ontario ~ Wokingham, England ~ Amsterdam
Bonn ~ Sydney ~ Singapore ~ Tokyo ~ Madrid ~ San Juan
Paris ~ Seoul, Korea ~ Milan ~ Mexico City ~ Taipei, Taiwan

About The Authors

Paula Rood gives inservice courses and workshops on process writing for all ages. She is a teacher at Nassakeag Elementary School in the Three Village Central School District in Setauket, New York. Lucrezia Iacomino is a special education teacher in the same school, teaching in a self-contained classroom.

Managing Editor:	Diane Silver
Senior Editor:	Lois Fowkes
Production Manager:	Janet Yearian
Production Coordinator:	Barbara Atmore
Production:	Gregor Nelson Design
Design Manager:	Jeff Kelly
Text Design:	Seventeenth Street Studios
Cover Design:	Rachel Gage
Illustrations:	Children at Nassakeag Elementary
	Gregor Nelson Design

Dedication

To David, for thirty-one years of loving patience, understanding, and encouragement;

To Tim, for being my first great accomplishment in life;

To Greg, for showing me how mountains can be conquered, if you have courage; and

To Caroline Sarah, the most special child in my life.

P.R.

To young and future writers everywhere.

L. I.

Acknowledgments

I would like to thank my many friends for helping me in so many ways, large and small: Pam and George Rice, Val Flora, Ruth Hawkins, Leslie Jungers, Tina Levine, Lorraine Cullen, Nancy Wigley, Robin Sicoli, Steve Graham, and Lisa George.

P. R.
June, 1992

Thanks to Jane Del Prete for holding the fort in my classroom to make my observations possible.

L. I.
June, 1992

~Contents

IV. Appendix

~Preface

The material presented in this book has been successfully used to teach writing to a wide range of age levels, from kindergartner through adult. The purpose for writing this book is to provide a literature-based, whole-language approach to:

~ organizing and managing a writers' workshop in an elementary school classroom
~ teaching writing skills to elementary school students

The Gift of Words has been divided into four parts:

Part I offers suggestions on setting up and managing the physical environment in which you will conduct your daily writers' workshop. The basic routines of a writers' workshop are introduced and defined: sharing, conferencing, responding, revising, editing, publishing, and celebrating.

Part II discusses the rationale for using children's literature as a teaching "tool" in a whole-language classroom. The lesson plan format is explained, and suggestions for using lessons are offered. Ideas for mini-lessons are included in this section.

Part III presents lesson plans that use children's literature to introduce and reinforce different aspects of writing. Each lesson uses a different, annotated selection of children's literature. A related bibliography that supports objectives follows each lesson.

Part IV, the Appendix, offers plans for organizing an in-house publishing company, ideas for book binding, instructions for making film strips, a sample writing award, a sample editor's checklist, and a whole-language bibliography.

~Introduction

Paula Rood

In the past 23 years of classroom teaching, I have been asked the following questions many times: "Paula, can you recommend a good book for...?" or "Paula, HOW do you get your students to write so well?"

The first question was always easy to answer. I can't remember a year in which I didn't find a way to integrate children's literature into different curriculum areas in my daily teaching. Therefore, I was always able to rattle off titles with enthusiasm. The second question, however, was somewhat perplexing.

Only recently, after considerable analysis of my approach to teaching writing, have I been able to recognize why my students have been so successful as writers. I realized that the program I had developed was, indeed, an on-going *process*. I did not limit listening, speaking, reading, and writing to encoding and decoding sounds and words or memorizing rules. Instead, I gave my students opportunities to learn to use language in an environment that allowed them to describe ideas related to their own life experiences.

Each day I shared a different selection of children's literature with my students, and with each selection I would highlight a different component or technique used in the process of writing. I did not isolate the teaching of writing or other content area skills and concepts into fragmented lessons. Children's literature became a language springboard, allowing me to combine content area skills and concepts into meaningful experiences.

I further realized that the environment I had created was supportive; it encouraged curiosity, questioning, experimentation, and risk-taking. The mutual trust that developed in such an environment was an essential ingredient in freeing students to express themselves.

Jean Little, author of children's literature, emphasizes the importance of our obligation as teachers to expose children to the richness of language. In a recent article, "A Writer's Social Responsibility" (*The New Advocate,* Vol. 2, Spring 1990), she states:

> Each of us is obliged to hold out to every child we meet, in person and in word, the gift of language....What a rewarding responsibility to be chosen to endow children with words. Polished words, words lovingly selected, beautiful, funny, challenging, lilting, harsh, sumptuous words....Without words children will be unable to think through life's subtle, sad, complex dilemmas; without words, they will not be strong enough to allow themselves and others grace and forgiveness. Wordless, they will not be freed to go forward into newness of life. Without words, there will not be stories.

Finally, by analyzing my program in terms of both process and environment, I was able to answer the question, "HOW do you get your students to write so well?" I had, indeed, met the obligation of which Jean Little speaks. I had endowed my students with words — their own words as well as the words of others — and celebrated their arrival as authors.

It is my hope that this book will serve as an inspiration to you as teachers to give students the "gift of language."

Lucrezia Iacomino

For the past seven years, I have worked with intermediate aged students with special needs. During my first year as a teacher with my own self-contained class, I was extremely frustrated by my inability to teach my students to write. They hated writing, and I was aware that the needs of my students were not being met in this important area. I attributed the problem to my own lack of experience.

To become a "more experienced" writing teacher, I attended several writing process workshops during that year; I read as much of the suggested literature on writing process as I was able to obtain; I became familiar with the basic tenets of the process approach to writing instruction and tried them with my students. Each attempt left me with the same feelings of frustration. The suggestions discussed in the literature and at the workshops geared to mainstream students were not effective when I used them with my students. Though I did considerable research, I was not able to find any materials that dealt with teaching writing process skills to students with special needs.

In the spring of that same year, I took another writing process course, this time conducted by Paula Rood. As the course progressed, she shared many writing samples produced by her second-grade students. I was impressed with their work, and once again I felt the familiar sense of frustration. How were these second-grade students able to produce quality writing? Why did they love to write? Paula must be doing something extraordinary in her writers' workshops; I needed to see for myself.

As part of the inservice course, participants were invited to observe Paula conducting writers' workshops with her second-grade students. Seeing her in action seemed like a way for me to solve my problem. At the end of the course, I asked Paula to allow me to observe her writers' workshop each day, beginning in September, and she agreed. Because we worked in the same building and had administrative approval, I was able to observe her approach to writing instruction from day one.

Each day, from September on, I observed and took notes. I then returned to my own class and modeled each lesson. I revised and adapted the lessons to meet the special needs of my students, and at last the bits and pieces of the writing process began to make sense, as I saw them in practice. I came to understand that the approach Paula was using was appropriate for *all* students, precisely because it is set up to meet students' individual needs, whatever they are.

In adapting Paula's lessons for my own students, first I focused on only one specific instructional objective at one time, presenting related information in short, logically sequential segments. I did not introduce a new concept or objective to the students until they had attained the previous one.

Second, I used a multimodal approach to instruction, beginning with the presentation of concrete visual stimuli and reinforcing them with auditory cues. I always provided activities and projects that included kinesthetic and tactile modes of learning as well.

Third, the children's literature, along with hands-on activities and projects, helped my students to successfully relate abstract concepts to concrete models as they worked at understanding and incorporating new concepts into their writing.

Fourth, writing became part of our daily schedule. Consistent review and daily practice of previously taught material aided students' recall. This strategy helped to facilitate comprehension of objectives that had been taught. The constancy and commitment to daily writing time, along with the structured environment of the writers' workshop helped my students to feel secure enough to attempt new projects and activities, all of which involved writing. Every project was completed, attractively published, and displayed.

Last, and perhaps most importantly, I provided my students with the "extra" time they required to grasp and internalize a new concept, technique, or skill. This was difficult, yet crucial to the successful publication of their work. My students took considerable time to complete a project. I worried about covering the material in the mandated curriculum. At times I felt as if we weren't making any progress. Could I justify this expenditure of time? As the year progressed, the answer was obvious: a resounding, "Yes!"

As students became comfortable with the writers' workshop format, their self-esteem rose to new heights, along with class pride. As each student published and celebrated his or her work, other classmates were motivated to do the same. Class books, in which each student had contributed at least one page, were extremely popular. Students checked these out and took them home to share and celebrate with their families. The pages of several of our class books became featured displays outside our school library before they were bound. My students were so proud to see their work prominently displayed.

In December one of my students had a poem and illustration published in our local newspaper. In the spring two others had their work published in a special edition of another local paper. The motivating force created by these accomplishments was contagious.

I had finally discovered an approach to writing instruction using sequential, literature-based lessons and activities that were appropriate and effective for all students at the elementary level, including students with special needs. As the year drew to a close, the old sense of frustration was gone, and I felt a need to share what I had learned with colleagues, especially new teachers.

The "writers' workshop" approach works; the classroom format offered in this book is simple; I encourage you to try it. The rewards for both you and your students will be well worth the effort.

I ~Launching a Writers' Workshop

"Come to the edge, he said. They said: We are afraid.
Come to the edge, he said. They came.
He pushed them . . . and they flew."
                                                    —Apollinaire

~Chapter 1

Setting Up a Special Sharing and Listening Area (Figure 1)

Before launching your daily writers' workshop you will want to arrange an area in the classroom where students will feel comfortable and safe when they are engaged in writing. The area you plan should be one in which your students feel secure in taking risks while attempting to communicate their feelings and thoughts through writing. In this area you and your students will begin to develop a community of young writers. You may wish to call this area the "Authors' Corner." Ideally, it will be just that: a corner of the room your students will learn to associate with listening, writing, and sharing.

Suggested equipment:

~ Area rug

~ Signs

~ Authors' chairs

~ Book rack

~ Table/boxes

~ Supplies

~ Editor's desk

~ Optional equipment

~Area rug   You may choose to use an area rug or carpet samples to define the area to be used for large group sharing. A rug creates a warm atmosphere in which students seem to feel comfortable and secure. (Stores may donate carpet samples to teachers, or parents may have area rugs they wish to donate.)

~Signs   Prior to "Launch Day," prepare three important signs. Display the three signs on bulletin boards or walls in the area you choose for sharing and listening. All signs should be colorful, legible, and highly visible.

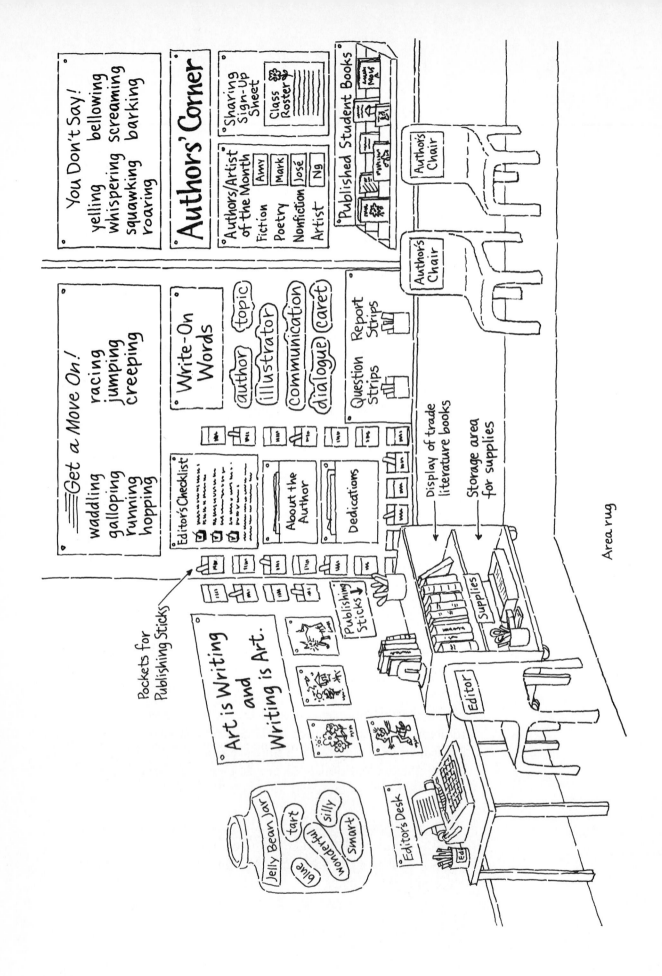

Sign 1: *Authors' Corner*

This is the largest and most prominent of the signs. Hang it above the book rack, bookcase, or shelf that you will use to display students' published writing.

Sign 2: *Art is Writing and Writing is Art*

From the start, this important message is heralded (Part III, Lesson 1). Students' art work is displayed beneath this sign.

Sign 3: *Write-On Words*

This is the sign under which you display the vocabulary words or phrases used during your daily writers' workshop sessions. You can come up with your own heading, but be sure to allot wall or board space to display important vocabulary words that will be introduced in each lesson. Prior to each lesson, prepare vocabulary strips for each word or phrase using colored construction paper (see Figure 1). Part I, Chapter 2 addresses the following displays shown in Figure 1: Authors and Artist of the Month, Sign up Sheet for sharing with other classes, and Question Strips storage pockets (see Part III, Lesson 14 for About the Author, and Lesson 3, Extended Activities for the Jelly Bean Jar, You Don't Say, and Get a Move On).

~Authors' chairs　　Two chairs should be placed in the sharing and listening area for authors, to use when sharing their writing with the class. These two chairs are to be used only for this purpose! To designate their importance, print two colorful signs, each saying "Author's Chair," and affix one to each chair with clear contact paper.

~Book rack　　Students' published writing should be prominently displayed and easily accessible. The same is true of trade literature, dictionaries, thesaurus, and other specialized books authors may need when writing. To facilitate this, equipment such as hanging book racks, standing bookcases, or shelves should be placed in the Authors' Corner.

~Table/boxes　　To complete the physical layout of your Authors' Corner, use a cart, table, stacked boxes, and so on to store materials and supplies. Keep in mind that students must have easy access to these supplies.

~Supplies　　The following supplies are useful:

Composition paper of varying sizes

Pencils

Colored markers and crayons

Scissors and pinking shears

Clear tape

Construction paper in various sizes and colors

Ink pads

Stapler

Clay

Fabric scraps

Yarn scraps

Glue

Hole punch

These supplies can be stored in labeled containers for easy management.

~*Editor's desk*   Provide an extra desk and two chairs so that students are aware of the importance of editing responsibilities when writing. Supply dictionaries, thesaurus, red/blue pencils for this station.

~*Optional equipment*   On a separate table a typewriter may be included, as well as a tape recorder, a film strip projector, earphones, computer.

~Chapter 2

Managing the Basic Routines of a Writers' Workshop

Teachers should become familiar with the basic routines of the workshop before "Launch Day." Following these routines will encourage student ownership of writing and help create a successful community of writers. The basic routines are

~ Reading Literature Selection

~ Writing Time

~ Sharing of Writing Through Conferencing

~ Responding to Writing

~ Writing, Revising, and Editing

~ Publishing and Celebrating Children's Writing

Plan to spend approximately thirty minutes each day in the writers' workshop. On most days, you will begin your session by reading a literature selection to your students. After discussing the literature selection with the group, students are given time to write. Students are never assigned topics! Instead, the technique introduced through the lesson is emphasized, and students are invited to try it out in their own writing. Teachers may find that some students need longer periods of time than others to get their thoughts down in writing. Reassure students that this is perfectly acceptable, and remind them that authors need to work at a pace that is comfortable for them as individuals. Students should be allowed (and encouraged) to work on their writing whenever they have free time, in school or at home.

It is also helpful to explain the routines and standards of behavior that students are expected to follow when engaged in the writers' workshop activities. Students have a dual responsibility: They are authors as well as members of an audience. As members of an audience, they must respect the ideas of others and help others to become better writers by actively listening and responding to each other's writing. Students are also expected to conduct themselves as you direct when working in the Authors' Corner. Initially, frequent reminders of the routines and expected standards of behavior may be necessary.

During writing time, it is important to circulate and confer with students, especially during the early weeks following your Launch Day. Teacher-directed conferences may be held with individuals, with small groups, or with the entire class, using the conference techniques discussed below. These techniques have been used with students of different age groups and abilities and are offered as a guide; use them to develop your own style and techniques.

When conferring with students, there are many ways in which a listener can respond.

~ It is often best to begin by inviting the student to speak first, to discuss the ideas that are now on paper. At this time, you may be able to help the student to define the topic, as well as discuss how the topic will be developed.

~ Next, with the information you've gained about the topic, ask the student's intent for further expansion of the topic.

~ Summarize what has been said by the author.

~ Paraphrase the author's writing by saying "I see in your writing that you . . . ." Offer positive comments that will encourage the student to focus on the chosen topic.

~ Ask questions about the topic that begin with the words, "Who, What, Where, When, Why, How," which will allow the student to recognize that more information may be necessary to clarify the writing in progress, or unnecessary information may have to be deleted.

In any case, you will enable your students to recognize that they, as authors, have options from which they can choose to change their writing through later revision.

(See Question Strips in "Writing, Revising, and Editing"; see Part III, Lesson 9.)

After you have spent time conferring with either individuals or small groups during writing time, invite the students to join you in the Authors' Corner for group sharing time. Select a few volunteers to take turns sitting in the Authors' Chairs and reading their writing in progress.

The Authors' Chairs are a very important part of the writers' workshop. When seated here, students begin to understand that their ideas, opinions, and writing are respected. As listeners, they also begin to assume the dual responsibility an author must have as writer and as a member of an audience. Using the Authors' Chairs will help to develop an atmosphere of trust while nourishing the sense of authorship a writer must have.

After each volunteer has shared, have the students join you in showing appreciation for what they have heard by applause, thumbs-up signals, and so on. At this point, you can model a conference about and response to each student's writing for a large group, using the techniques suggested earlier. Invite the class or author to:

~ Define the topic

~ Discuss the intent

~ Summarize or paraphrase the topic or intent

~ Offer positive comments and questions

Remind the students to be both positive and specific in their remarks. "I liked the story" or "It was nice" are not enough. Tell students that they should jot down words, phrases, or sections that are particularly exciting or descriptive in order to be able to comment on them after the piece has been read.

As soon as you feel comfortable with the format of conference/response you've developed with your students (as individuals, in small groups, and with an entire class), you may want to begin training them to assume the role of listener for their peers in conferences they can conduct on their own. As many teachers already know, a class of eager young authors vying for a teacher's attention can become overwhelming. Student-directed peer conferences can help alleviate this problem. Students may conduct these conferences in pairs or in small groups of 3–5 students.

In peer conferences, students share their writing with a partner or a small group of peers without the teacher's direction. The techniques remain the same. The listener comments positively on what was read and then proceeds to ask the questions that will help to clarify, expand, and revise the piece, just as they did in the teacher-directed conferences. Questions generated are written on Question Strips by the listening partner(s). Students are encouraged to save these Question Strips for possible later use (see Question Strips in "Writing, Revising, and Editing"; see Part III, Lesson 9).

Parents as well as students from upper grades can be invited to work with younger students during the writers' workshop. If you choose to have either parents or older students participate, plan on having them attend several workshops as trainees so that they become familiar with response and questioning techniques. Their help will leave you free to work with individuals or small groups of students who may be experiencing specific problems.

Writing, Revising, and Editing

Once the stage has been set and students begin to write, there seems to be no end to their output. By allowing your students the freedom to choose their own topics and time each day to write about what is important to them, you have begun to empower them with ownership. The literature you read each day during the writers' workshop further enhances this sense of ownership. Your students will begin to make the connection between their own attempts at writing and the literary styles, genres, and techniques you have introduced during your workshop lessons.

Keeping track of students' writing in progress can be time consuming and confusing. To alleviate potential problems, here are a few suggestions:

~ Provide students with individual writing folders that are filed alphabetically in a labeled box. The box can be stored in the Authors' Corner, but should be easily accessible. If you choose to use this system you will want to provide your students with composition paper of various sizes for their writing in progress.

~ Have students use a hardcover notebook. Notebooks can be stored in students' desks or in a designated storage box in the Authors' Corner.

~ Provide students with one or more of the following stamps: "Rough Draft," "Writing in Progress," "Date." Stamps and ink pads can be purchased at office supply stores.

During the first week of the writers' workshop, be sure to explain to your students the system you have chosen so that they understand how and where they are to store their writing in progress. (See Part II, "Ideas for Mini-Lessons.")

One frequently asked question is "How do you choose what gets published?" The answer is relatively simple: you don't. The student chooses! Through daily writing, sharing, and conferring, students quickly assume a strong sense of ownership (control over their topics), as well as how much or how little they wish to tell their audience about these topics. Feedback from a variety of audiences helps to clarify these ideas. Students eagerly respond to suggestions, and are encouraged to revise. Publishing becomes a goal.

Students may not always be able to remember all of the ideas and suggestions they've heard during the revision process. One possible solution is to use Question Strips. These are strips of paper on which the audience members write down questions and comments about the piece of writing they've just heard. The strips are kept in the student's hardcover writing book or are clipped to the piece of writing. Question Strips help the student during the revision process. They serve as reminders that may be addressed in order to clarify or expand a piece of writing. Blank Question Strips are stored in an oaktag pocket in the Authors' Corner. (See Figure 1 and Part III, Lesson 9.) Students are encouraged to use them during writing time each day.

Editing responsibilities are introduced as soon as your first student announces, "I'm ready to publish!" Criteria for publishing are dependent upon age and grade level. Initially, young students (second grade) might be expected to assume the following editing responsibilities:

~ Begin all sentences with a capital letter.

~ End each sentence with appropriate punctuation.

~ Underline any words that may be misspelled.

As students develop additional skills they can be expected to assume further responsibilities in the editing process (use a dictionary to correct spelling errors, use quotation marks to show dialogue, and so on).

Once you have decided on the criteria for student editing, an Editor's Checklist can be displayed in the Authors' Corner (see Figure 2 and sample Editor's Checklist in the Appendix). This checklist can remind students of the responsibilities they must meet prior to submitting the piece for final editing by an adult. As new skills are acquired, the Editor's Checklist can be updated. Final proofreading and editing remain the task of adults, either a teacher, parent volunteers, or trained upper-grade students.

Figure 2

Editor's Checklist

❑ I have shared with at least five different audiences.

❑ I have revised and used the caret (^).

❑ I have edited with another person to correct spelling and punctuation. I underlined words that need spelling corrections.

*Place a publishing stick in your pocket if you have completed all the items on the checklist.

Keeping up with the editing demands of an entire class can become overwhelming if management is not efficient and orderly. You may use Publishing Sticks stored in pocket cards. Publishing Sticks are tongue depressors on which the following reminders are written: "I've shared. I've revised. I've edited." (See Figure 3.) Prepare one Publishing Stick for each student. Store the Publishing Sticks in a labeled can in the Authors' Corner, near the Editor's

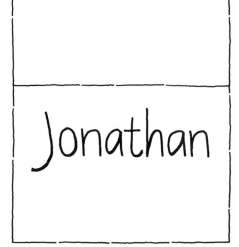

Figures 3 and 4

Checklist. Next, pocket cards, labeled with each student's name, should be stapled onto the same board on which the Editor's Checklist is displayed. (Library card pockets may be used or made from oaktag. (See Figure 4.)

As soon as it becomes apparent that students understand their responsibilities in the writing process (sharing, holding conferences, revising, and editing), gather the class together for a mini-lesson that will introduce them to Publishing Sticks. When students are ready for final editing by an adult, they place a Publishing Stick in their oaktag pocket. Remind them that they can signal the teacher with a Publishing Stick only *after* they have met the following responsibilities:

~ "I've shared." Students must share with a variety of audiences (individual, small groups, entire class). As the piece progresses, each listener initials the piece after it is shared. The teacher may want to suggest that students choose different listeners for each sharing so that students do not favor just one type of audience.

~ "I've revised." The student adds or deletes words, phrases, or sentences to expand and clarify ideas. At this point students can be introduced to the *caret* (^). Teaching students how to use this tool to revise their text eliminates the need for unnecessary recopying. (See Part III, Lesson 5 on use of the caret.)

~ "I've edited." Students use the established criteria for editing in the Editor's Checklist that is displayed in the Authors' Corner. It is helpful to have students use colored pencils when editing their work. Younger students usually find editing easier if they work with a partner. (See Figure 1, Figure 2, and Sample Editor's Checklist in the Appendix.)

Teachers may also want to designate one writers' workshop session per week as Publishing Day. During the writers' workshop on this day, meet with those authors who are ready to publish. Parent volunteers and upper-grade students can be invited to the classroom on Publishing Day to assist with the final editing.

While individual students are meeting with adults, the remaining students are writing, sharing, holding conferences, or revising their work in progress.

Publishing and Celebrating Students' Writing

Once the final editing process has been completed, students are within reach of their goal: having their writing published!

The publishing method you offer can be plain or fancy, simple or complex. A piece of construction paper with the title and student's name written on it can be stapled to the newly edited text to constitute a published book. At the opposite end of the spectrum, you could set up a school publishing company that would offer lamination and binding. The amount and availability of time, money, and volunteers will influence the publishing methods you choose to offer. (See Appendix: "Bookbinding Instructions" and "How to Start an In-School Publishing Company.")

Most of the time you will be publishing individual student's books. However, occasions may arise when whole class collaborative efforts may be published, too.

Students can decide whether they want their writing published in a small or large book, a bound or stapled book, a ready-made blank book, and so on. In primary grades, adults can print or type the final copy. Intermediate students may be capable of assuming this task themselves. Space should be allotted for illustrations on the printed or typed pages. After the printing or typing is completed, the students can

~ Add illustrations

~ Design a cover and title page

~ Add an About the Author page (See Part III, Lesson 14)

~ Add a Dedication page

Remember that publishing is not an end. Rather, it is a means to an end: putting student writing into the hands of readers and celebrating their arrival as authors.

As soon as each student is published, have a special sharing session in the Authors' Corner. At this time, the student reads his or her book while seated on the Author's Chair. After a show of appreciation and positive comments have been made, the student places the book on the display rack for all to enjoy.

Author	Mon. 10:00 a.m. Mrs. Takahashi	Tues. 12:00 a.m. Mr. Ramirez	Wed. 11:15 a.m. Ms. Black	etc. →
Sara A.		✓		
Juan B.				
Rashida C.	✓			
Ruibo D.			✓	
Michael S.				

Figure 5 *Sample Sharing Sign-Up Sheet*

Students' writing should be accessible to audiences beyond the peers in their classrooms. One way to accomplish this is to allow students to share their writing with other classes. To arrange these sharing sessions with other classes, you can send a questionnaire to your colleagues. Be sure to include your own class schedule. When questionnaires are returned, transfer the information to a class roster as indicated in Figure 5. Make several copies of this sheet (one for each week) and staple the copies under a colorful sign that says "Sharing Sign-Up Sheet." Each Monday, a helper tears off last week's sheet and writes the date of the present week in the designated space. Students are then invited to sign up for the classes they would like to visit that week by checking (√) the appropriate boxes.

Other suggestions for sharing students' published writing with a variety of audiences include the following:

~ Arrange an Authors' Day (or Night) with parents or other classes.

~ Display books in the school library.

~ Display books in the main office.

~ Publish pieces in school or local newspapers.

~ Videotape children reading their pieces during the school year. Invite parents to school to view the tape or send it home for viewing.

~ Set up an Authors' Sharing Tree (see Figure 6).

~ Arrange to have books displayed in your local community library.

~ If you have access to a button-making machine, prepare Author Buttons (see Figure 7).

~ Design a logo for your publishing company and include it in student books (see Figure 8).

Figure 6 *Left: Authors' Sharing Tree before students have begun to publish.*

Right: Authors' Sharing Tree after students have published.

Each student is given a mini-book (3"x4" oaktag folded in half). Title and author are written on cover. Students choose two illustrations from published book and reproduce them inside the mini-book with appropriate captions.

Student writing can be celebrated in other ways, too. After several weeks of writers' workshop, prepare a sign announcing Authors and Artist of the Month (see Figure 1) and display it in the Authors' Corner. Include the following categories:

~ Author of Fiction

~ Author of Nonfiction

~ Author of Poetry

~ Artist

Each month poll your students by written ballot to determine the three outstanding authors and one outstanding artist for that month. Make up a new ballot each month (see Figure 9).

Display the winners' names under the Authors and Artist of the Month sign. Gold foil awards are affixed to the selected books (see Figure 10). Each child should have the opportunity to be an award winner. Therefore, children cannot receive a second in the same category until every child has received *at least one* award.

Other possibilities of celebrating student writing include

~ Preparing filmstrips and audio tapes of published books (see Appendix)

~ Having students prepare biographical sketches (see Part III, Lesson 14, "About the Author")

~ Having students prepare dedications

~ Having students choose favorite pieces and collate them into a class book

~ Giving out writing awards (see Appendix)

Figure 7 *Metal Button*

Figure 8 *Sample logo*

~ Having students design a logo for the class publishing company to include on the title page of each book published (see Figure 8).

Launch Day can be any day you choose. Ideally, it will be sometime during the first week of school. If you decide to begin your program later in the year, you may want to build student anticipation and interest prior to that day by displaying colorful signs or balloons advertising that "Launch Day is Coming on (date)!" Displaying a countdown calendar is another suggestion.

Experience has shown it to be most helpful to involve parents in writers' workshop activities from the very start. Prior to Launch Day, send a letter home to parents and ask that each child be provided with the following materials: pencils, crayons, markers; scissors; clear tape; glue; a ruler; a large can in which to store these materials; a notebook for writing (a black and white hard cover composition notebook is suggested). In the same letter you may also want to explain briefly the daily routines you have established for your writers' workshop. Once parents understand the process in which their children are engaged (daily writing, sharing, holding conferences, revising, and editing) as well as how they can help their child meet the responsibilities you've established, they become more actively involved. If your school has an Open House or Back to School evening for parents, you can explain your writers' workshop in person.

Figure 9 *Sample Ballot for Authors and Artist of the Month*

Fiction	Author	Artist
Two Birds by Anita Sanchez	❑	❑
My Dog by Keiko Watanabe	❑	❑
The Princess by Jason Stein	❑	❑
Nonfiction		
My Dad's Car by John Kim	❑	❑
The Zoo by Ann Rait	❑	❑
Poetry		
Birds by Sue Ng	❑	❑
The Snowman by Rashida Brown	❑	❑

Directions: Vote for one fiction author, one nonfiction author, one poet, and one artist.
*There can only be four checks (√) on your balllot.

Figure 10

Parents can be a tremendous help in other ways, too.

~ Supplying publishing materials (see Appendix for sample letter)

~ Preparing fabric- or wallpaper-covered books in which children's writing is published (see Appendix for sample letter)

~ Transcribing students' edited writing into prepared blank books

~ Typing students' edited writing

~ Making sound filmstrips of students' published writing (see Appendix for sample letter)

~ Attending writers' workshops as a writing partner (see Chapter 2: "Sharing Students' Writing Through Conferences")

Considerations for Students with Special Needs

Please bear in mind that the suggestions offered in Part I should be adapted to suit the needs of each class. If you are teaching a class of special needs students, the following information may be helpful.

1. Students are likely to experience greater success in writing if they choose their own topics, yet due to many factors (e.g., limited intellectual and academic abilities, lack of motivation and self confidence), many students with special needs find it difficult to decide what to write. Artwork can be a means of topic selection and expansion. Assure students that they need not show anyone their drawings. A class-generated, collective list of topics from which each student can choose would be another way of helping reluctant writers and artists to generate topics. Jot down ideas as you listen to students talk during the day and add to the list. Invite students to help you categorize these ideas.

2. Physical movement of materials is sometimes difficult for students with special needs. It can help to provide specific, structured, step-by-step directions appropriate for your own students in setting up your writers' workshop area.

3. If one or two students have not completed a project, allow them to work on it to closure to give credence and value to their work and to the project. It can also be more efficient for students to have a continuous block of time for their project, rather than having to stop and start too often.

Postitive Outcomes of the Writers' Workshop Approach

1. Students of many ability levels can be engaged in the same activity.

2. Cooperation improves students' expressive language as they learn to compliment and support each other's work.

3. Students' listening comprehension improves as they listen to hear others respond to their writing, and also to hear their own suggestions incorporated into their peers' work.

4. More positive social relationships are fostered.

5. Students' attitude toward reading improves because the teacher is seen as a reader and a writer.

6. Listening to entertaining stories, using them as models, and getting special recognition for completed work motivates students to write, and to succeed.

For further information about writing process classrooms and whole-language classrooms, see the Whole-Language Bibliography in the Appendix.

II ~Using Children's Literature in a Whole-Language Classroom

The art of teaching is the art of assisting discovery.
—Mark Van Doren

~Chapter 3

Children, Literature, and Whole Language

Using literature in an elementary classroom is not a new idea. Most often, teachers use story time as a pleasant way to entertain their students. What is new, however, is the notion that children's literature can be used as an effective teaching tool. When used in this manner, children's literature can help students to develop and reinforce literacy skills in many areas of language usage: critical thinking, speaking, listening, reading, and writing. Children's literature presents ideas about our world in a way that is easily understood by young people and is relevant to them. In addition, the authors of children's literature use writing techniques that are universal and serve as models for young authors to emulate.

Yet many teachers, especially those teaching intermediate students, still question the appropriateness of using children's literature as a teaching tool. They may say: "My students have already heard (or read) that book," or "My students will think that book is too young for them." Age and grade level should not be viewed as a barrier when deciding whether or not a piece of literature is appropriate for use in a classroom. Instead, choose literature because:

~ It highlights specific aspects of the writing process or highlights specific writing techniques.

~ It is highly readable and appeals to readers and listeners of all ages.

~ It has been used successfully in lessons with students ranging in age from age six to adult.

The classroom environment teachers create for their students is of utmost importance. Your respect and enthusiasm for a piece of literature will be recognized by your students and they, in turn, will respond positively. Literature written by Eric Carle, Ann Jonas, Henrik Drescher, and Vera Williams (to name a few) has been used in lessons for young adult (and adult) students. Their enthusiastic response to these authors was a delight to behold! On the other hand, students as young as six years old have responded to the rhythm of language and the message communicated by Walt Whitman, Emily Dickinson, Robert Frost, Langston Hughes, and other authors of "adult literature."

Much of the recent enthusiasm supporting the use of literature as a teaching tool can be attributed to the concurrent rise in usage of whole-language teaching methodologies. The following definition of *whole language* is offered by the Bureau of English and Reading Education of the New York State Education Department in its 1989 position paper:

> Whole language is not a methodology but a philosophy, the major premise of which is that language should not be separated into its component parts but is best learned through use in authentic situations that have meaning for the learner. The following beliefs about language, learning, and the learner also serve as cornerstones of the whole-language philosophy:
>
> ~ Children learn not merely by imitation or rote, but by constructing their own meaning from the world around them.
>
> ~ The young learner's reading and writing skills develop simultaneously.
>
> ~ Language learning flourishes in an environment that is supportive of risk taking and exploration.
>
> ~ Errors are evidence of a learner's efforts to make sense of his or her world.
>
> ~ Language is used for a variety of purposes and audiences that influence the form of communication.
>
> ~ Reading, writing, listening, and speaking are language processes that complement and support each other.
>
> ~ Becoming a skillful reader requires many encounters with natural, complete text.
>
> ~ Becoming a skillful writer requires many opportunities to produce whole communications.
>
> ~ All of the linguistic cue systems (e.g., grammar, sound, meaning) are at work during any instance of language use.
>
> ~ The purpose of language instruction is to help students use language skillfully and not solely to learn language skills.

In short, whole language is a philosophical stance that says language instruction across the curriculum should be guided by teachers' observation of students engaged in meaningful language use. In such a program, language learning depends on an integration of reading, writing, listening, and speaking. The learner uses language for a variety of purposes and audiences, encounters complete pieces of text, produces meaningful types of communication, and learns in a supportive environment that encourages risk taking. Not only is children's literature one of the most effective tools for teaching language/communication skills, it also provides the means for integrating those skills into other curriculum areas.

~Chapter 4

How to Use Lesson Plans

In Part III, you will see how the Authors' Corner and the basic routines of the writers' workshop are used on a daily basis. By following the order of the lessons suggested below, an environment of total language involvement may be created.

Part III contains twenty-eight lesson plans, each focusing on a different selection of children's literature. Some selections are used to introduce and reinforce important aspects of the writing process, such as topic selection, topic expansion, story elements, revision, and editing. Other selections introduce and reinforce specific writing techniques, such as repetition, dialogue, comparisons, and use of descriptive language. *It is strongly recommended that teachers familiarize themselves with the selection and lesson objectives before beginning each lesson.*

For those teachers not familiar with whole-language and writing- and reading-process approaches to teaching, it is suggested that Lessons 1–10 be taught in the order presented. Lessons 1–10 introduce the basic ingredients for story development in a sequential manner and will establish a foundation for other writing skills to be taught at a later date.

Teachers familiar with whole-language philosophies and writing and reading processes may find it more convenient to use only those lessons that will accomplish objectives in the programs they have already established. (Although I usually cover all of the remaining lessons presented in Part III [Lessons 11–28] during the course of a school year, I have never taught them in the same order in 20 years of teaching. P.R.)

Allow students' writing to guide you, taking into account interest level in choice of topics, techniques used in writing, areas of weakness or strength, and so on.

Please keep in mind the importance of reinforcement. *Five to ten days* may be spent developing each lesson's objectives. Each day after the introductory lesson, you may share a different literature selection during writers' workshop. (See the Related Bibliography following each lesson.) These subsequent books reinforce the objectives introduced, and the extra days provide time for students to practice new writing techniques. *Remember, though, time parame-*

ters for developing each lesson's objectives are open-ended and will vary from class to class depending on age level, needs, and schedule demands.

Thematic writing, author studies, and genre studies are not emphasized in these lessons. Instead, it is more important for children to develop a strong sense of ownership through their own writing. Using a variety of authors, styles, techniques, and genres helps to accomplish this. Once this sense of ownership has begun to emerge, introduce genre; thematic writing is best introduced through content area units.

Lesson Plan Format

The structural pattern of each lesson is repeated in order to facilitate familiarization with writers' workshop routines. Each lesson in Part III has been organized using the following format:

Literature Selection: The specific title, author, and book's publisher

Summary: A brief explanation of the book's content

Objectives: The skills and concepts to be used in the lesson

Vocabulary: Key words or phrases used during the lesson in order to achieve the objectives

Getting Ready: Materials and directions needed for the lesson

Step-by-Step Activities: The lesson's content, sequentially developed

Related Bibliography: Alternative books that support the lesson's objectives

Extended Activities: Ideas for the expansion of the objectives in some lessons

Throughout each lesson, words the teacher could use appear in italics. These are suggested for oral discussion; they are not intended to be used as a script. Teachers using this program are encouraged to use whatever language they find most comfortable when addressing their students.

It is hoped that you find these lessons helpful and that you and your students discover writing to be an exciting challenge.

~Chapter 5

Ideas for Mini-Lessons

Establishing routines and paying attention to the details of organization and management are very important.

When introducing new programs to students, teachers may in many instances overlook the details or assume that students have prior knowledge of them. In a writers' workshop program, seemingly familiar terms such as *title page* or *fiction* may be overlooked on the assumption that students know what they mean. Answers to questions such as "Where do I store my writing materials?" or "How do I use a stapler?" are sometimes presumed to be self-evident. They should not be.

Many teachers and students have had prior experience using writing-process workshop ideas and are familiar with a variety of teaching styles and organizational and management techniques. Others, both students and teachers, have not had prior exposure. Consider using mini-lessons to introduce or reinforce any or all of the ideas listed below as suggestions.

Mini-lessons are short and to the point and offer much flexibility, including the following features:

1. They do not have to be presented sequentially.

2. Order and frequency of reinforcement are determined by teacher/student needs.

3. Time parameters are determined by teacher/student needs. (Kindergarten teachers may devote an entire writers' workshop to mini-lessons on how to use and store colored markers; intermediate-level teachers may focus on the parameters of audience behavior; second- and third-grade level teachers may need to review the meaning of the term *title page*.)

4. Once a mini-lesson has been presented it can be reinforced quickly and as often as needed.

5. Mini-lessons can be incorporated into writers' workshop time parameters or can be done at another time during the teaching day. More than one mini-lesson can be introduced at a time, according to students' needs and abilities.

Some suggestions for mini-lessons:

~ Identify parts of a book (author, illustrator, title page, dedication, table of contents, chapters, index, bibliography).

~ Explain the difference between fiction and nonfiction.

~ Discuss the use and management of materials found in the Authors' Corner (see Part I, Chapter 1).

~ Explain how and where to store student writing materials, writing in progress, and so on (see Part I, Chapter 2, "Responding to Students' Writing").

~ Discuss how and when to get ready for publishing (see Part I, Chapter 2, "Writing, Revising, and Editing").

~ Identify behavior expectations in a writers' workshop (see Part I, Chapter 2, "Managing Routines").

~ Point out the dual responsibilities of an author in the role of a writer and as a member of the audience (see Part I, Chapter 2, "Managing Routines").

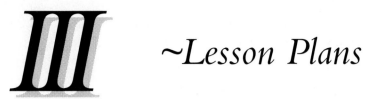

~Lesson Plans

Children need models more than they need critics.
—Joubert

~Teacher's Notes

Lessons 1 to 10 help students to develop topics in a sequential manner. Lessons 11 to 28 focus on technique and style. For all lessons, please remember the following points:

~ Prior to reading the literature selection, draw students' attention to the book's front matter, and read the title page and dedication aloud.

~ Whenever possible, point out art media and techniques used by the illustrator, and their connection to the purpose or mood of the literature selection.

~ The amount of time allotted for writing will vary according to age and grade level expectations as well as lesson objectives.

~ Circulate among students as they write, conferring with as many as possible while providing support and encouragement (see Part I, Chapter 2).

~ The objectives of each lesson are usually reinforced by reading additional literature selections to students over a period of several days (see Related Bibliography after each lesson).

~ Students must be allowed time to experiment in their own writing each day.

When students have returned to the Authors' Corner after writing time, they may volunteer to share new pieces of writing based on the lesson, writing in progress based on previous lessons, completed pieces of writing they are ready to publish, or artwork they wish to expand through writing.

Place any vocabulary strips used during each lesson in the Write-On Words section of the Authors' Corner bulletin board (see Figure 1).

~Lesson 1

Literature Selection

SIMON'S BOOK
Henrik Drescher
New York: Lothrop, Lee & Shepard, 1983

Summary

Simon draws a picture of a monster who crawls off the drawing board and becomes the topic of the story that unfolds.

Objectives

~ To use art as a primary source of topic selection for writing

~ To understand the connection between writing and art as basic means of communication

~ To feel part of a community of writers

~ To review any mini-lessons previously taught (see Part II, Chapter 5, "Ideas for Mini-Lessons")

Vocabulary

~ author

~ illustrator

~ communication

~ topic

~ "Art is writing and writing is art."

Getting Ready

Prepare vocabulary strips (see Chapter 1, "Setting up a Special Sharing and Listening Area"). Assemble the following materials:

~ crayons and markers

~ 9-by-12-inch drawing paper

Step-by-Step Activities

1. Invite students to join you at the Authors' Corner. Once students are gathered at the Authors' Corner, welcome them and explain that the writers' workshop is a special daily activity that will help them to become better writers.

2. Introduce new vocabulary. One at a time, display the vocabulary strips. Ask:

What do you think this word means?

Accept all reasonable answers before defining each vocabulary word.

Ask students if they can think of different ways ideas and feelings are communicated (telephone, sign language, TV, newspapers, books).

Explain that in the writers' workshop, important ideas are called *topics.* A topic is the main idea authors communicate to their readers.

3. Prior to reading *Simon's Book,* ask:

Can anyone predict what the topic is?

Can anyone predict what characters we'll meet?

Can anyone predict where the story will take place? Can anyone predict the time of year? Can anyone predict the time of day?

4. Read the story to students. Suggestions for discussion:

What is the topic of the book? (a friendly monster)

Who are some of the characters we meet? (Simon, the monster, the pens)

Where and when does the story take place? (in Simon's bedroom, late at night)

Who is the author in the story? (Simon)

How did Simon choose to communicate his ideas about his topic? (He drew his story.)

Display the vocabulary strip "Art is writing and writing is art." Tell students:

Simon did not write his story, he drew it. Art and writing are ways in which people communicate their ideas. Artwork tells a story much the way words can paint a picture in our minds.

by Joyce K.

by Natalie

Figure 11 *Although the two students have chosen the same topic (a house), their artwork is completely different, and the ideas they choose to communicate about their artwork will be different, too.*

5. Prior to having students return to their work areas for writing time, tell them:

Today you will have a chance to communicate your ideas through art, just as Simon did in his story.

Think of things about yourself that you would like to communicate to your audience. Possibilities include information on family members, pets, where you live, your favorite foods, your hobbies, places you've visited, dreams you'd like to see come true, and so on.

Distribute 9-by-12-inch drawing paper and have students return to their work areas to begin their artwork.

6. After ten to fifteen minutes, have students rejoin you at the Authors' Corner. Have them bring their drawings with them. Drawings do not have to be completed at this point. Children can work on them whenever they have free time. Ask for volunteers to share the ideas about themselves that they are working on. Have students sit in the Author's Chair while sharing. Encourage questions and comments from the audience.

Emphasize that although many students have drawn pictures of the same topics, each author/artist has a different story to share (see Figure 11). Tell students that the ideas they have communicated through their artwork will become topics for their writing (see Figure 12).

At the end of the lesson, collect the artwork. Tell students that their drawings will be used at the next writers' workshop, and encourage students to ask for and complete the drawings during free time.

Related Bibliography

These books also support the lesson objectives and could be used in place of *Simon's Book.*

Broger, Achin, and Michele Sambin. *Francie's Paper Puppy.* Natick, Mass.: Picture Book Studio, USA, 1984.

Figure 12 *Artwork that could be turned into topics for later expansion into stories.*

Ginsberg, M. *Ookie Spooky*. New York: Crown, 1979.

Goffstein, M. *A School of Names*. New York: Harper & Row, 1986.

Kesselman, Wendy. *Emma*. Illustrated by Barbara Cooney. New York: Harper & Row, 1980.

Mrs. McNeil's Kindergarten Friends. *Looking for a Rainbow*. Worthington, Ohio: Willowisp Press, 1987.

Raskin, Ellen. *Nothing Ever Happens on My Block*. New York: Macmillan, 1989.

Tampert, Ann. *Grandfather Tang's Story*. New York: Crown, 1990.

Williams, Vera. *Cherries and Cherry Pits*. New York: Greenwillow Books, 1986.

Extended Activity

Confer with children while they are drawing and jot down the topics they have chosen. Then make a list of topics generated by all students that day, leaving plenty of space on the sheet for additional topics. Put the list into students' folders or attach it to their writing notebooks before the next writers' workshop and invite students to add to the list as new topics come to mind. The list can be revised from time to time if you wish.

~Lesson 2

Literature Selection

CHERRIES AND CHERRY PITS
Vera Williams
New York: Greenwillow Books, 1986

Summary

Bidemmi loves to draw pictures about people and events in her life. Her artwork serves as an impetus to writing.

Objectives

~ To expand artwork topics through writing

~ To review Lesson 1 objectives

~ To review mini-lesson objectives

Vocabulary

~ expand

Getting Ready

Prepare a vocabulary strip (see Chapter 1, "Setting up a Special Sharing and Listening Area").

Step-by-Step Activities

1. Invite students to join you at the Authors' Corner. Distribute the drawings students completed in Lesson 1. Once students are gathered at the Authors' Corner, review the objectives and vocabulary from the previous lesson:

In our last writers' workshop, we saw how Henrik Drescher used art to communicate his topics.

Does anyone remember what the word topic *means?*

Does anyone remember how Simon communicated his topic? (He drew the monster.)

2. Introduce new vocabulary:

Today we are going to learn how art can help us expand *our topics through writing.*

Display the vocabulary strip:

What do you think the word expand *means?*

Accept all reasonable answers before defining the word.

3. Prior to reading *Cherries and Cherry Pits,* ask:

Can anyone predict what the topic is?

Can anyone predict what characters we'll meet?

Can anyone predict where the story will take place? Can anyone predict the time of year? Can anyone predict the time of day?

Can anyone recognize the art technique Vera Williams used to illustrate the book? (markers)

4. Read the story to students. Suggestions for discussion:

What is the topic of the book? (how Bidemmi draws her stories)

Who are some of the characters we meet? (Bidemmi, the people who live in her building, her family)

Where and when does the story take place? (in Bidemmi's city neighborhood in recent times)

Explain that Bidemmi first identifies her topic by drawing it; she then expands her topic through writing.

5. Ask for volunteers to share the artwork they did during Lesson 1. Say:

You will be expanding the topics you have chosen in the same way that Vera Williams had Bidemmi expand her topics.

Your drawings contain many topics about which you can write.

6. Prior to having students return to their work areas for writing time, tell them:

Today in your writing, you may want to try expanding the topics in your artwork just as Vera Williams did in Cherries and Cherry Pits, *the book we have just finished reading.*

7. After the allotted time for writing, have students rejoin you at the Authors' Corner. Ask them to bring along any writing they would like to share with the group.

Related Bibliography

The books in the Lesson 1 Related Bibliography also support the lesson objectives and could be used in place of *Cherries and Cherry Pits.*

Extended Activity

Create your own Hooray for Us class book. Using students' artwork and writing from Lessons 1 and 2 as a guide, ask students to think of many varied and unusual responses to complete this phrase: I am my _____ (see Figure 13). Distribute 9-by-12-inch light-colored construction paper and allow your students to choose their favorite art medium to illustrate one of their ideas. After your students have completed their illustrations, help them mount their artwork on 12-by-18-inch black construction paper. Help your students to revise and edit their phrases before copying them onto strips of writing paper. Attach the strips to the artwork and publish as a book.

Figure 13 *Front cover for class book,* Hooray for US!

Sample pages of children's work from class book, Hooray for US!

~Lesson 3

Literature Selection

CHILDREN'S ZOO
Tana Hoban
New York: Mulberry Books, 1985

Summary

After listing three or four adjectives and then naming a specific animal, Tana Hoban creates a vivid description of zoo inhabitants that complements her black-and-white photographs.

Objectives

~ To expand topics through the use of specific details as a writing technique
~ To use nouns and adjectives to expand topics
~ To review Lesson 1 and Lesson 2 objectives

Vocabulary

~ detail
~ specific
~ noun
~ adjective

Getting Ready

Prepare vocabulary strips (see Chapter 1, "Setting up a Special Sharing and Listening Area").

1. Invite students to join you at the Authors' Corner. Once students are gathered at the Authors' Corner, review objectives and vocabulary from the previous lesson:

In our last writers' workshops, we learned how different authors choose topics and expand them.

Does anyone remember what topic *and* expand *mean?*

2. Introduce new vocabulary:

Today we are going to learn how authors use specific details to expand their topics.

One at a time, display the vocabulary strips:

What do you think this word means?

Accept all reasonable answers before defining each vocabulary word.

3. Prior to reading *Children's Zoo,* ask:

Can anyone predict what the topic is?

Can anyone predict what characters we'll meet?

Can anyone predict where the story will take place? Can anyone predict the time of year? Can anyone predict the time of day?

Can anyone recognize the art technique Tana Hoban used to illustrate the book? (Photos—you may want to explain that photography is an art form that can be used to illustrate and communicate ideas, thoughts, and feelings.)

4. Read the story to students. Suggestions for discussion:

What is the topic of the book? (animals in a zoo)

Who are some of the characters we meet? (elephant, seal, zebra) *These words are nouns.*

Does anyone remember the words Tana Hoban used to describe the [name any animal from the book]? (Answers will vary.) *These words are called* adjectives. *Tana Hoban used adjectives to expand her nouns (animals). Adjectives have added* specific details *to her writing. They have painted a picture with words.*

5. Prior to having students return to their work areas for writing time, say:

Today in your writing, you may want to try expanding your writing by using adjectives, just as Tana Hoban did in Children's Zoo, *the book we have just finished reading.*

6. After the allotted time for writing, have students rejoin you at the Authors' Corner. Ask them to bring along any writing they would like to share with the group.

Related Bibliography

These books also support the lesson objectives and could be used in place of *Children's Zoo.*

Baylor, Byrd. *Everybody Needs a Rock.* Illustrated by Peter Parnall. New York: Aladdin Books, 1982.

Cambell, Rod. *Dear Zoo.* New York: Macmillan, 1982.

Heller, Ruth. *A Cache of Jewels.* New York: Grosset and Dunlop, 1987.

————. *Many Luscious Lollipops.* New York: Grosset and Dunlop, 1989.

Neumeir, Marty, and Byron Glaser. *Action Alphabet.* New York: Greenwillow Books, 1984.

Rosen, Michael. *We're Going on a Bear Hunt.* New York: Macmillan, 1989.

Ross, David. *A Book of Hugs.* New York: Thomas Y. Crowell, 1980.

Extended Activities

1. Have your students write adjective-noun list poems using Tana Hoban's *Children's Zoo* as a model. Write names of animals on small pieces of paper and have each student choose one. Tell students not to share the identity of the noun with anyone. After the students have written their list poems, they can share them and invite the audience to guess their animal. Ask students to list many varied and unusual adjectives to describe their noun just as Tana Hoban did in her book. Some suggestions for discussion include: color, shape, size, texture, how the animal moves, how it eats, and how it communicates. Distribute one piece of 9-by-12-inch light-colored construction paper to each student and allow each one to choose his or her favorite art medium to create a picture of the animal. (Tissue paper collage works well with this activity.) Trim the completed artwork and mount it on 12-by-18-inch black construction paper. Help students revise and edit their adjective-noun list poems before copying them on writing paper strips and attaching the strips to the artwork (see Figure 14). Collate the finished pieces in ABC order using the animal's name (aardvark, bear, cat, and so on) and publish them as *Our Class Zoo Book.*

Figure 14

Note: The theme can be any topic with strong visual properties—animals, fruit, vegetables, weather, holiday treats, and so on.

2. As a homework assignment, ask your students to write adjectives on the Delicious Adjectives sheet (see page 41). Tell them that the adjectives must be spelled correctly. Primary students may get help from adults, and older students may use a dictionary. The next day, create an adjective work bank and display it in your Authors' Corner. Have your students copy their adjectives on colored paper cutouts of jelly beans and attach them to a large cutout of a jar (see Figure 1 and Figure 15). Delicious Adjectives sheets may be kept in the students' writing journals or writing folders. Encourage the students to find additional adjectives each night so that you can fill your jelly bean jar.

Note: You may want to supply real jelly beans for your class to enjoy while doing this activity. Be sure to obtain parents' permission in case of allergies, medications, or other restrictions.

3. Create a Jelly Bean Adjective Dictionary for your class. The dictionary will help to avoid duplication of adjectives already found on the jelly bean jar word bank and will reinforce alphabetical order skills. To prepare the blank dictionary pages, fold ruled sheets of writing paper into four columns and assign two columns to each letter of the alphabet. Label the columns to make dictionary pages. Each day, have students enter their new adjectives into the class dictionary. Remind students that they must first check the entries to be sure the adjectives they are adding have not been entered by another student.

Delicious Adjectives

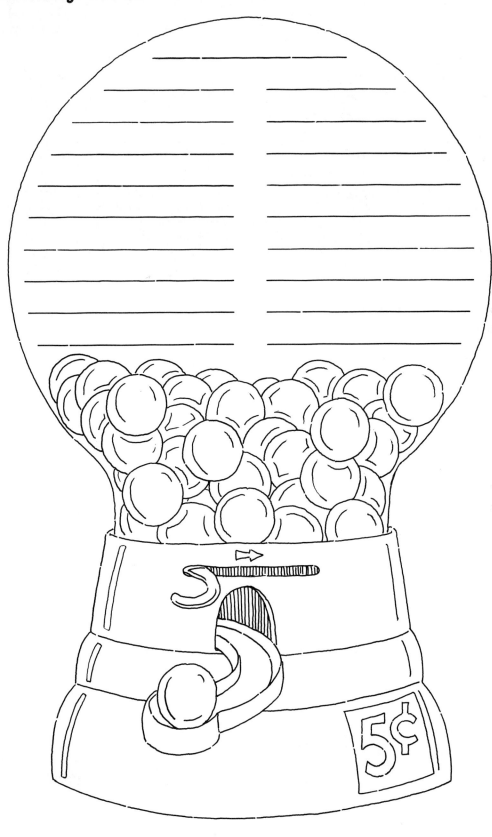

Jelly Bean Jar

little yummy new great moldy tart
green big good old brown
crazy yellow spicy weird round
gross black grape slimy
sneaky crunchy rotten
spooky gooey tasty pink
silly sour small fat
chewy red soft tasty tiny
slick bitter haunted sweet
rough white giant

"Get A Move On" Words

swimming	stamping
galloping	skateboarding
skipping	biking
crawling	marching
leaping	skating
dancing	running
flying	driving
swinging	prancing
slithering	riding
jogging	walking

"You Don't Say" Words

growling	oinking	squeaking
squawking	tweeting	meowing
roaring	chattering	singing
trumpeting	crowing	clucking
chirping	buzzing	peeping
shouting	barking	crying
talking	purring	howling
hissing	screaming	whining
neighing	yelling	whispering
hooting	mooing	shrieking

Figures 15 and 16

4. Create a gerund word bank to display in your Authors' Corner (see Figure 1 and Figure 16). Gerunds are adjectives that end in -*ing*.

5. Create a word bank using words that tell us how different animals communicate with each other. Display the word bank in your Authors' Corner (see Figure 1 and Figure 16).

~Lesson 4

Literature Selection

EMMA
Wendy Kesselman
Illustrated by Barbara Cooney
Garden City, New York: Doubleday, 1985

Summary

Motivated by a birthday gift, a 72-year-old woman begins to paint.

Objectives

~ To understand that revision is a writing responsibility

~ To expand, rearrange, or delete text when revising

~ To use the caret (^) as a revision tool

~ To use the Question Strip as a revision tool and as a management technique (see Part I, Chapter 1)

~ To review objectives of Lessons 1–3

Note: This literature selection, *Emma,* can also be used for Lesson 5 and Lesson 6. It is suggested that teachers of primary students spend at *least* three sessions developing the ideas in these lessons. Each lesson may be further reinforced through additional mini-lessons based on individual class needs, using the Related Bibliography or your own selections. Teachers of older students may be able to present all of the new information in one writers' workshop, as long as everyone can keep pace.

Vocabulary

~ revise

Getting Ready

Prepare a vocabulary strip.

Step-by-Step Activities

1. Invite students to join you at the Authors' Corner. Once students are gathered at the Authors' Corner, review the objectives and vocabulary from the previous lesson:

In our last writers' workshop, we learned how authors and artists expand their topics using specific details. Does anyone remember what these words mean?

2. Introduce new vocabulary:

Today we are going to learn how authors sometimes change or revise a piece of writing so that readers will better understand it.

What do you think the word revise *means?*

Accept all reasonable answers before defining the vocabulary word.

3. Prior to reading *Emma,* ask:

Can anyone predict what the topic is?

Can anyone predict what characters we'll meet?

Can anyone predict where the story will take place? Can anyone predict the time of year? Can anyone predict the time of day?

4. Read the story to students. Suggestions for discussion:

What is the topic of the book? (Emma paints scenes of her youth the way she remembers them.)

Who are some of the characters we meet? (Emma, her family, and her pet cat)

Where and when does the story take place? (in her house, recent times)

Why doesn't Emma like her birthday gift? (The painting doesn't reflect the way she remembered her childhood village.)

How does Emma solve the problem? (She eliminates details she doesn't like and paints her own versions of her village.)

Does Emma share her revised versions of the village with anyone? (yes)

What are their reactions? (They are delighted, because the artwork Emma produced told her story, not the story of others.)

5. Prior to having students return to their work areas for writing time, say:

Today in your writing, you may want to try changing writing you have already done by revising it, just as Emma revised her paintings in the book we have just finished reading.

6. After the allotted time for writing, have students rejoin you at the Authors' Corner. Ask them to bring along any writing they would like to share with the group.

Related Bibliography

These books also support the lesson objectives and could be used in place of *Emma*.

Broger, Achin. *Francie's Paper Puppy*. Natick, Mass.: Picture Book Studios, 1986.

Nixon, Joan Lowry. *If You Were a Writer*. New York: Macmillan, 1988.

Williams, Vera. *Cherries and Cherry Pits*. New York: Greenwillow Books, 1986.

~Lesson 5

Literature Selection

See Lesson 4 or choose a new title from the Lesson 4 Related Bibliography to continue developing the objectives.

Objectives

~ See Lesson 4.

Vocabulary

~ caret

Getting Ready

Prepare a vocabulary strip.
Have available a 24-by-36-inch sheet of chart paper.

Step-by-Step Activities

1. Invite students to join you at the Authors' Corner. Once students are gathered at the Authors' Corner, review objectives and vocabulary from the previous lesson:

In our last writers' workshop, we learned how authors sometimes change or revise their writing. Does anyone remember what revise *means?*

2. Introduce new vocabulary:

Today we are going to learn how writers use a caret (^) *to revise their writing.*

Display the vocabulary strip:

What do you think the word caret *means?*

Accept all reasonable answers before defining the vocabulary word.

3. Prior to reading, decide whether to review *Emma,* choose a book from the Related Bibliography, or choose your own book. If you choose a new title, use the questions from Lesson 4 (Step 3).

4. If you have chosen a new book, read the story to students. If you have not chosen a new book, or if you have extra time, you may wish to share a drawing and some writing of your own. Copy your story on a large sheet of chart paper.

My Cat
Written and Illustrated by Mrs. Rood

I have a cat. I love my cat. My cat is great. My cat is cute.

Take this opportunity to review and reinforce sharing responsibilities (see Chapter 2, "Sharing Children's Writing Through Conferences"). Ask students to comment positively on the art and writing. Typical responses include: "I have a cat, too," "I can tell the color of your cat," "I like the adjective 'cute.'" Ask students if they need to know more. Students usually ask, "What is your cat's name?" The following is a possible response:

That's a good question. I haven't included that detail in my story, have I? I need to include that information. I must revise my story. Remember, changing a story by adding words, taking words out, or rearranging words is called revision. Where do you think my new detail should go? (Accept all reasonable suggestions for revisions.) I have a problem because I can't fit all the new words in the space. However, I can use a caret in revising the writing.

Demonstrate the use of a caret in revising the writing.

My Cat
Written and Illustrated by Mrs. Rood
①
I have a cat. I love my cat. My cat is great. My cat is cute.
① Her name is Tinkerbell.

5. Prior to having students return to their work areas for writing time, tell them:

Today in your writing, you may want to try using a caret to revise a piece of writing you've done, just as I did in my story.

6. After the allotted time for writing, have students rejoin you at the Authors' Corner. Ask them to bring along any writing they would like to share with the group.

....

Related Bibliography

(See Lesson 4.)

~Lesson 6

Literature Selection

See Lesson 4 or choose a new title from the Lesson 4 Related Bibliography to continue developing the objectives.

Objectives

~ See Lesson 4.

Vocabulary

~ Question Strip

Getting Ready

Prepare a vocabulary strip.
Have available 2-inch-wide strips of writing paper for Question Strips.

Step-by-Step Activities

1. Invite students to join you at the Authors' Corner. Once students are gathered at the Authors' Corner, review objectives and vocabulary from the previous lesson:

In our last writers' workshop, we learned how writers sometimes use a caret to revise their stories. Does anyone remember what a caret is?

2. Introduce new vocabulary:

Today we are going to learn how to use a Question Strip *to help us revise a piece of writing.*

Display the vocabulary strip:

What do you think a Question Strip is?

Accept all reasonable answers before defining the vocabulary phrase.

3. Prior to reading, decide whether to review *Emma,* review your own revised writing used in the previous lesson, review a student's revised writing, or choose a new book from the Lesson 4 Related Bibliography. If you choose a new title, use the questions from Lesson 4 (Step 3).

4. Introduce Question Strips (see Chapter 2, "Writing, Revising, and Editing" for a complete explanation).

5. Prior to having students return to their work areas for writing time, tell them:

Today in your writing, you may want to try using a Question Strip while revising your writing with a partner.

6. After the allotted time for writing, have students rejoin you at the Authors' Corner. Ask them to bring along any writing they would like to share with the group.

Related Bibliography

(See Lesson 4.)

~Lesson 7

Literature Selection

PANCAKES, PANCAKES!
Eric Carle
Saxonville, Mass.: Picture Book Studios, 1990

Summary

It's very early in the morning and Jack is so hungry that what he really wants is a large pancake for breakfast.

Objectives

~ To become familiar with the basic ingredients, or elements, found in the beginning of a story (topic, characters, setting, time, mood)

~ To use the basic story ingredients (elements) in writing

Note: This literature selection, *Pancakes, Pancakes!* may be used for Lessons 7, 8, and 9. It is suggested that teachers of primary students spend at least three sessions developing the objectives of these lessons. Each session may be further reinforced through additional mini-lessons based on individual class needs. You may use books from the Lesson 7 Related Bibliography, or choose your own selections. Teachers of older students may be able to present all of the information in one writers' workshop, as long as everyone can keep pace.

Vocabulary

~ setting

~ time

~ mood

~ basic ingredients

~ sequence

~ beginning

~ words signalling sequence: before, after, next, then, finally, first, second, third

~ recipe

Getting Ready

Prepare vocabulary strips.

Have available a 24-by-36-inch sheet of chart paper for Basic Story Ingredients chart (see Figure 17).

Step-by-Step Activities

1. Invite students to join you at the Authors' Corner. Once students are gathered at the Authors' Corner, review objectives and vocabulary from the previous lesson:

In our last three writers' workshops, we learned how a writer can revise a story by using carets and Question Strips. Does anyone remember what revise, caret, *and* Question Strip *mean?*

2. Introduce new vocabulary:

Today we are going to learn how a writer can organize and revise a story following a special recipe.

One at a time, display the vocabulary strips:

What do you think this word means?

Figure 17

Basic Story Ingredients

Beginning
    topic
    characters
    setting and time
    mood

Middle
    problem identified

End
    problem solved

Accept all reasonable answers before defining each vocabulary word.

What are the basic ingredients I'd need to make a peanut butter and jelly sandwich? (bread, peanut butter, and jelly)

What tools or utensils would I need? (knife)

How would I make the sandwich? (Accept all reasonable answers.) *We call this special order a* sequence.

What are the basic ingredients a writer might need to write a story? (Accept all reasonable answers.)

3. Prior to reading *Pancakes, Pancakes!* ask:

Can anyone predict what the topic is?

Can anyone predict what characters we'll meet?

Can anyone predict where the story will take place? Can anyone predict the time of year? Can anyone predict the time of day?

4. Read the story to the students. Suggestions for discussion:

What is the topic of the book? (Jack's mother teaches Jack how to make a pancake.) *Writers must use basic ingredients, too. One basic ingredient needed to begin a story is an idea, or topic.*

Who are the important characters we meet? (Jack and his mother)

Important characters are usually introduced in the beginning *of a story. They are basic ingredients, too.*

Where do we meet Jack and his mother? (at home on their farm) *This basic ingredient is called a story's* setting. *Writers usually place their characters in a specific place in the beginning of a story.*

What is the time of day or time of year? (Accept all reasonable answers.)

What is Jack's mood? (impatient because he is hungry) *Writers usually establish a specific time and create a mood in the beginning of a story. Setting, time, and mood are basic story ingredients.*

Before continuing the discussion, display the Basic Story Ingredients chart you have prepared (see Figure 17). Refer to the chart as you review the beginning of *Pancakes, Pancakes!*

5. Prior to having students return to their work areas for writing time, tell them:

Today in your writing, you may want to try using the basic ingredients to begin your story, or you may want to revise the beginning of a piece of writing you have already done.

6. After the allotted time for writing, have students rejoin you at the Authors' Corner. Ask them to bring along any writing they would like to share with the group.

Related Bibliography

These books also support the lesson objectives and could be used in place of *Pancakes, Pancakes!*

Baylor, Byrd. *Everybody Needs a Rock*. New York: Aladdin Books, 1974.

McGovern, Anne. *Stone Soup*. Illustrated by Winslow Pinney Pels. New York, Scholastic, 1968.

Note: A recipe or "how to" lesson can be applied to Lesson 7 objectives.

Extended Activities

1. Have students summarize and then illustrate a story they have written using the Story Trail (see pages 54 and 55).

2. Prepare a generic recipe, leaving blank spaces for ingredients and supplies. Instruct students to fill in the information needed to complete the recipe for their favorite breakfast, lunch, dinner, dessert, or snack. You might want to plan a Super Sundae party for the entire class, allowing your students first to write the recipes for their favorite sundae and then to actually create their sundaes. Help your students revise and edit their recipes and then publish them as a book.

Note: Be sure to obtain parents' permission in case of allergies, medications, or other restrictions.

After you write your story, draw pictures to illustrate the "Basic Ingredients."
Cut out cards and paste them in order along the story trail.

3

Next ...

2

First ...

1

Title

Author

Illustrator

Fold back and glue.

6

Finally ...

5

Then ...

4

After that ...

Story Trail

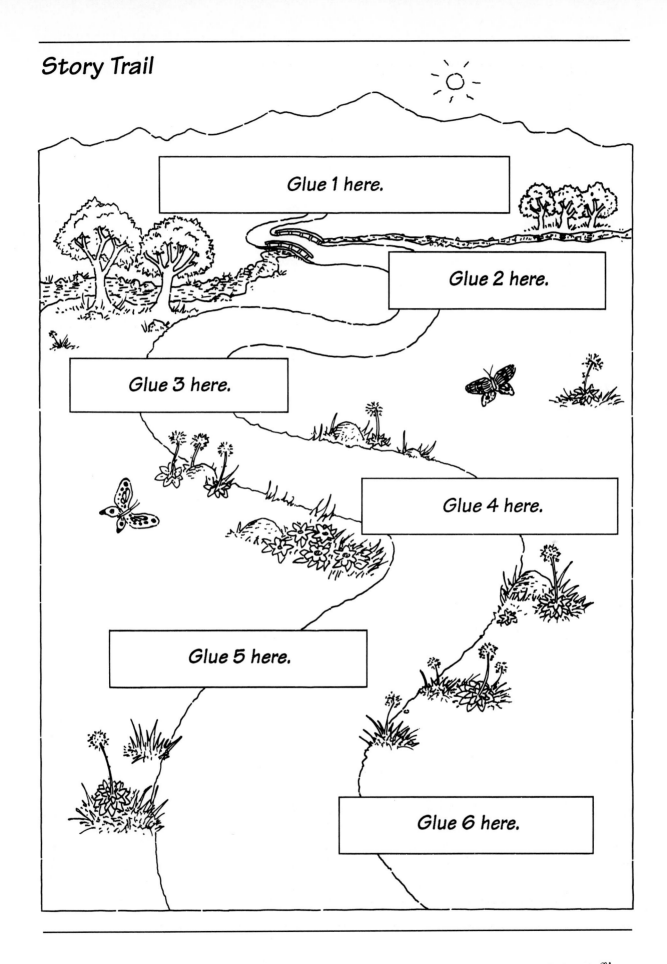

~Lesson 8

Literature Selection

See Lesson 7 or choose a new title from the Lesson 7 Related Bibliography to continue developing the objectives.

Objectives

~ To become familiar with the basic ingredients or elements found in the middle of a story (problem identification)

~ To use the basic story ingredients (elements) in writing

Vocabulary

~ middle

~ problem

Getting Ready

Prepare vocabulary strips.

Display the Basic Story Ingredients chart (see Figure 17).

Step-by-Step Activities

1. Invite students to join you at the Authors' Corner. Once students are gathered at the Authors' Corner, review objectives and vocabulary from the previous lesson:

In our last writers' workshop, we learned that a story follows a special order, or sequence: the beginning, middle, and end. We also learned that a topic, characters, time, setting, and mood are basic ingredients found in a story's beginning.

Review vocabulary words introduced in the previous lesson as necessary.

2. Introduce new vocabulary:

Today we are going to learn the basic ingredient of a story's middle.

One at a time, display the vocabulary strips and ask students if they know what the word means. Accept all reasonable answers before defining each vocabulary word.

3. Prior to reading, decide whether to review the book used in the previous lesson, choose a student's writing, choose your own selection, or choose a book from the Lesson 7 Related Bibliography. If you choose a new title, use the questions from Lesson 7 (Step 3).

4. Read the story to students. Refer to the Basic Story Ingredients chart prepared for Lesson 7 (see Figure 17). If you are using *Pancakes, Pancakes!,* proceed with the following suggestions. If you are not, substitute information for each question relating to the story you have chosen to read.

Who can remember the topic of Pancakes, Pancakes!*?* (Jack's mother teaches Jack how to make a pancake.)

Is this a problem for Jack's mother? (Yes, because Jack is impatient but doesn't know how to make a pancake by himself.)

Writers create problems *in their stories. Once a problem has been identified, we move into the* middle *of a story.*

5. Prior to having students return to their work areas for writing time, tell them:

Today in your writing, you may want to try using the basic ingredients to write the beginning and middle of your story, or you may want to revise the middle of a piece of writing you've already done.

6. After the allotted time for writing, have students rejoin you at the Authors' Corner. Ask them to bring along any writing they would like to share with the group.

Related Bibliography

(See Lesson 7.)

~Lesson 9

Literature Selection

See Lesson 7 or choose a new title from the Lesson 7 Related Bibliography to continue developing the objectives.

Objectives

~ To become familiar with the basic ingredient, or element, found at the end of a story (solution of problem)
~ To use basic story ingredients (elements) in writing

Vocabulary

~ solution
~ end

Getting Ready

Prepare vocabulary strips.
Display Basic Story Ingredients chart (see Figure 17).

Step-by-Step Activities

1. Invite students to join you at the Authors' Corner. Once students are gathered at the Authors' Corner, review objectives and vocabulary from the previous lesson:

In our last writers' workshop, we learned the basic ingredient of a story's middle part: a problem must be identified.

Review any vocabulary words introduced in the previous lesson as necessary.

2. Introduce new vocabulary and ask the students what they think each word means. Accept all reasonable answers before defining each new vocabulary word.

3. Prior to reading, decide whether to review the book used in the previous lesson, choose a student's writing, choose your own selection, or choose a book from the Lesson 7 Related Bibliography. If you choose a new title, use the questions from Lesson 7 (Step 3).

4. Read the story to students. Suggestions for discussion:

How did Jack and his mother solve their problems? (Jack's mother sends Jack to get all the pancake's ingredients. Then she assembles all the ingredients on the kitchen table and follows a recipe. Jack finally gets to have breakfast.)

Refer to the Basic Story Ingredients chart as you review the objectives of this lesson.

Writers use problem solutions as a basic ingredient in their stories. Problems are usually solved at the end of a story. Use the basic story ingredients in the order in which they are listed on our chart. This special order is called story sequence.

5. Prior to having students return to their work areas for writing time, tell them:

Today in your writing, you may want to try using the basic ingredients to write the end of your story, or you may want to revise the end of a piece of writing you've already done.

6. After the allotted time for writing, have students rejoin you at the Authors' Corner. Ask them to bring along any writing they would like to share with the group.

Related Bibliography:

(See Lesson 7.)

~Lesson 10

Literature Selection

THE MITTEN
Jan Brett
New York: G. P. Putnam and Sons, 1989

Summary

In this beautifully illustrated retelling of an old Ukrainian folk tale, a boy loses one of the mittens his grandmother has knitted for him and then finds it, much to his surprise.

Objectives

~ To reinforce objectives of Lessons 1–9

Vocabulary

~ See Lessons 1–9.

Getting Ready

Prepare vocabulary strips.

Step-by-Step Activities

1. Invite students to join you at the Authors' Corner. Once students are gathered at the Authors' Corner, review objectives and vocabulary from the previous lesson:

In our last writers' workshop, we learned how an author uses Basic Story Ingredients to expand a topic and then to revise the story. Review words introduced in Lessons 1–9 as necessary.

2. Introduce any words not previously introduced in Lessons 1–9. One at a time, display vocabulary strips:

What do you think this word means?

Accept all reasonable answers before defining each vocabulary word.

3. Prior to reading *The Mitten,* ask:

Can anyone predict what the topic is?

Can anyone predict what characters we'll meet?

Can anyone predict where the story will take place? Can anyone predict the time of year? Can anyone predict the time of day?

4. Read the story to students. Suggestions for discussion:

What is the topic of the book? (a missing mitten)

Who are some of the characters we meet? (grandmother, animals)

Where and when does the story take place? (countryside during winter)

What mood is established? (happy)

What problem was first identified? (The boy loses his mitten but doesn't realize it's gone. After the last animal, the mouse, crowds into the mitten, the bear needs to sneeze.)

How is the problem solved? (the bear sneezes, throwing the mitten into the air)

How does the story end? (The boy, returning home, sees the mitten float down to the ground.)

5. Prior to having students return to their work areas for writing time, say:

Today in your writing, you may want to try a mitten story of your own. Use the basic ingredients you have learned, just as Jan Brett did in The Mitten, *the book we have just finished reading.*

6. After the allotted time for writing, have students rejoin you at the Authors' Corner. Ask them to bring along any writing they would like to share with the group.

Related Bibliography

These books also support the lesson objectives and could be used in place of *The Mitten.*

Kellogg, Steven. *The Mystery of the Missing Red Mitten.* New York: Pied Piper Books, 1974.

Rogers, Jean. *Runaway Mittens*. Illustrated by Rie Mukoz. New York: Greenwillow Books, 1988.

Thomas, Patricia. *"Stand Back," Said the Elephant, "I'm Going to Sneeze!"*. Illustrated by Wallace Trip. New York: Lothrop, Lee & Shepard, 1971.

Tresselt, Alvin. *The Mitten*. Adapted from the version by E. Rachev. Illustrated by Yaroslava. New York: Lothrop, Lee & Shepard, 1964.

Extended Activity

Using colored construction paper, trace and cut out one pair of 2-by-3-inch mittens for each of your students. Draw an outline of a large mitten on a 36-by-60-inch sheet of paper. Ask your students to think of many varied and unusual animals who may have hidden in the mitten. Distribute 6-by-9-inch pieces of construction paper and ask your students to draw their favorite animal. Have your students cut out their animals and glue their mittens on the animal's "hands." Attach the completed artwork to the large outlined mitten (see Figure 18). Encourage your students to use their new ideas to write their own mitten stories.

Figure 18

~Lesson 11

Literature Selection

THE QUICKSAND BOOK
Tomie de Paola
New York: Holiday House, 1977

Summary

Using a humorous fictional format, de Paola has his main character rescue someone from quicksand, but not before teaching the
reader facts about quicksand.

Objectives

~ To review objectives of Lessons 1–9

~ To apply Lesson 7, 8, 9 objectives to expository (nonfiction)
  writing

~ To become familiar with management and organizational
  techniques

Note: You may wish to spend several sessions developing the
objectives in this lesson. Use the generic questions found in
Suggestions for Discussion for each additional lesson, but relate
them to different literature selections. The Extended Activity
should be introduced after students demonstrate an understanding
of the first and second objectives of this lesson.

Vocabulary

~ nonfiction

Getting Ready

Prepare a vocabulary strip.

1. Invite students to join you at the Authors' Corner. Once students are gathered at the Authors' Corner, review objectives and vocabulary from the previous lesson:

In our last writers' workshop, you used the basic story ingredients to help you become better authors.

Review words from previous lessons as necessary. It will be helpful to use the Basic Story Ingredients chart during this lesson (see Figure 17).

2. Introduce new vocabulary:

Today we are going to learn how authors use basic story ingredients in nonfiction *writing.*

Display the vocabulary strip:

What do you think the word nonfiction *means?*

Accept all reasonable answers before defining the vocabulary word.

3. Prior to reading *The Quicksand Book,* ask:

Can anyone predict what the topic is?

Can anyone predict what characters we'll meet?

Can anyone predict where the story will take place? Can anyone predict the time of year? Can anyone predict the time of day?

4. Read the story to students. Suggestions for discussion:

What is the topic of the book? (A girl falls into quicksand.)

Who are some of the characters we meet? (Jungle Girl, Jungle Boy)

Where and when does the story take place? (jungle, recent times)

What is the mood? (humorous though dangerous)

What problem is identified? (Girl doesn't know how to get out of quicksand.)

How is the problem solved? (Boy ["expert"] rescues her, but only after delivering a lecture on quicksand.)

Did Tomie de Paola write a fiction or nonfiction book? (Both! The story unfolds using fictional elements, but the facts about quicksand are true, or nonfiction.)

When writing about nonfiction topics, the author must still use basic story ingredients, but must think about a different kind of problem: How can I teach my audience about the topic I've chosen? The nonfiction author's problem is solved by presenting all the facts about a particular topic.

Tomie de Paola chose fictional characters and setting to teach us about a nonfiction topic, quicksand.

5. Prior to having students return to their work areas for writing time, say:

Today in your writing, you may want to choose a nonfiction topic. Ask yourself questions about your topic. Think of questions an audience might ask if you were an expert on your topic, just as Tomie de Paola did in The Quicksand Book, *the book we have just finished reading.*

6. After the allotted time for writing, have students rejoin you at the Authors' Corner. Ask them to bring along any writing they would like to share with the group.

Related Bibliography:

These books also support the lesson objectives and could be used in place of *The Quicksand Book.* Any nonfiction book presenting factual material about a specific topic could be used. Any of Aliki's "how to" books are strongly suggested, including *How a Book Is Made, Dinosaur Bones, Corn Is Maize.*

The books listed below use fictional format to teach readers facts about the real world, just as Tomie de Paola did in *The Quicksand Book.*

Cole, Joanna. *The Magic Schoolbus Inside the Earth.* Illustrated by Bruce Degen. Scholastic, 1987.

———. *The Magic Schoolbus at the Waterworks.* Illustrated by Bruce Degen. Scholastic, 1986.

———. *The Magic Schoolbus Lost in the Solar System.* Illustrated by Bruce Degen. Scholastic, 1988.

de Paola, Tomie. *The Popcorn Book.* New York: Scholastic, 1978.

Locker, Thomas. *Where the River Begins.* New York: Dial, 1984.

Ryder, Joanne. *Chipmunk's Song.* New York: Dutton, 1987.

———. *The Snail's Spell.* New York: Puffin Books, 1988.

———. *Where Butterflies Grow.* New York: Dutton, 1989.

Extended Activities

These activities are designed to be presented to the entire class, using a common topic to be researched by all. The activities can be adapted to smaller groups or to individuals.

Since research reports usually take more time to develop than fiction writing does, plan on spending several sessions developing the ideas presented below. Once students have had time to use these techniques, you'll find they become quite adept at doing independent research and writing.

Before the first session, assemble the following supplies: one sheet of 36-by-60-inch chart paper, 3-by-5-inch cards (200–300), or a large supply of writing paper strips (200–300), cellophane tape, one folder or envelope for each student to store cards or strips they use, and books on the topic from school, community, or personal libraries.

Ask your students to write the topic you've chosen on one card (demonstrate). Encourage students to ask questions about the topic that they might want to write about in the report. You may have to model several questions at this point: *What are rocks? Where do they come from? How are they made?* and so on. Direct students to write each question they generate on a separate 3-by-5-inch card or strip of paper.

At this point, you may wish to allow students to continue to generate questions independently. Remind students to write one question per card, and have them store the cards in the envelope you have provided. If you choose to continue modeling the lesson, do so until the supply of questions seems exhausted. Tape the resultant question cards to the 36-by-60-inch sheet of chart paper. Be sure all cards ask a different question. Do not use duplicates. If students have worked independently on different topics, allow them space to spread out their cards or strips.

Choose any question and ask if someone can think of a heading or category it would belong under. For example, "Do rocks have minerals in them?" might go under the heading "How Rocks Are Made" or "Ingredients of Rocks." Find all other questions that would fit that category and move those cards to a new area under their new heading. Continue subdividing the remaining question cards into new categories until all the original cards are placed in new areas. Students working independently would now clip together piles of category cards in preparation for independent research.

Research can now begin. To prepare, gather as many books on the topic as you can and place them in an area of your room that is easily accessible to students. Independent small groups or individuals may go to the library to get their own books.

Working in small groups or on their own, students now read books, searching for answers to the questions they have written on cards. Answers they find are then written on the back of the question card or strip. Cards and strips should remain in categories.

Once all questions have been answered, students are ready to write their reports using their categorized cards as a guide.

~Lesson 12

Literature Selection

Storm in the Night
Mary Stolz
New York: Harper & Row, 1988

Summary

While a storm rages outside his house, a young boy's fears are soothed by listening to his grandfather's story.

Objectives

~ To review story development: introduction of characters and setting

~ To use the five senses to establish setting and mood

~ To use dialogue to develop characters

Vocabulary

~ five senses (see, hear, smell, feel, taste)

~ dialogue

Getting Ready

Prepare vocabulary strips.

Step-by-Step Activities

1. Invite students to join you at the Authors' Corner. Once students are gathered at the Authors' Corner, review objectives and vocabulary used for Lesson 7:

Does anyone remember what the basic ingredients for a story are? (See Figure 17.)

Does anyone remember what characters, time, setting, *and* mood *mean?*

2. Introduce new vocabulary:

Today we are going to learn how an author uses the five senses *and* dialogue *to place characters in a setting and create a mood.*

One at a time, display the vocabulary strips:

What do you think this word means?

Accept all reasonable answers before defining each vocabulary word.

3. Prior to reading *Storm in the Night,* ask:

Can anyone predict what the topic is?

Can anyone predict what characters we'll meet?

Can anyone predict where the story will take place? Can anyone predict the time of year? Can anyone predict the time of day?

4. Read the story to students. Suggestions for discussion:

What is the topic of the book? (a storm; a boy's fears)

Who are some of the characters we meet? (the boy, his grandfather, the cat)

Where and when does the story take place? (one summer night in the boy's house)

What mood is created? (fear)

How does the author communicate this information? (by using her senses of sight, smell, and sound to describe the action of the storm and characters)

Mary Stolz has drawn a picture with words. She allows us to see in our minds all that is taking place in her story.

How does the author develop the rest of the story? (through a series of questions asked by the boy and answered by the grandfather)

Two characters engaged in a conversation is called a dialogue. *By using dialogue, authors can communicate much about their characters by allowing the characters to be themselves.*

5. Prior to having students return to their work areas for writing time, say:

Today in your writing, you may want to try using your five senses and dialogue to communicate your ideas, just as Mary Stolz did in Storm in the Night, *the book we have just finished reading.*

6. After the allotted time for writing, have students rejoin you at the Authors' Corner. Ask them to bring along any writing they would like to share with the group.

Related Bibliography

These books also support the lesson objectives and could be used in place of *Storm in the Night*.

Briggs, Raymond. *The Snowman*. New York: Random House, 1978.

Burnett, Frances H. *The Secret Garden*. New York: Scholastic, 1987.

Cherry, Lynn. *The Great Kapok Tree*. New York: Harcourt Brace Jovanovich, 1990.

Martin, Bill, Jr. and John Archambault. *Knots on a Counting Rope*. Illustrated by Ted Rand. New York: Holt, 1987.

Rylant, Cynthia. *Night in the Country*. New York: Bradbury Press, 1986.

Yolen, Jane. *Owl Moon*. Illustrated by John Schoenherr. New York: Putnam, 1987.

~Lesson 13

Use a book from the Lesson 12 Related Bibliography or any you feel meets the lesson objectives.

Note: Begin Lesson 13 by following the Lesson 12 format up to Step 5 of the Step-by-Step Activities section.

5 (new). Prior to having students return to their work areas for writing time, say:

Today we are going to try a new writing activity. [You may call this the Writers' Warm-Up and compare it to an athlete's warm-up exercises.] *I want you to get ready by sharpening all five senses.*

I want you to imagine yourselves in a specific place, during a specific season or time of day, and see, hear, smell, taste, and feel what is happening.

Have students return to work areas for writing. Say:

Begin your warm-up by quickly writing three words to tell where you are, the time of year or day, and your mood. (Example: beach, afternoon, happy)

Now use your senses to help you expand your idea to explain what you see, hear, smell, feel, and taste. (Example: "I heard waves splashing and laughter as I ran in the sand. I was so hot I couldn't wait to reach the water!")

Allow five minutes for this warm-up activity. Caution students that they are *not* writing a complete story but merely warming up by exercising their senses. Most students need several of these warm-up periods before they feel comfortable with the exercise.

After five minutes, have students join you in the Authors' Corner with their warm-up writing. Ask volunteers to share what they've written without naming the place, time, and mood they originally wrote down. The audience is invited to guess the specific time, place, and mood by listening to the descriptive words the author has used, much as you would if creating a riddle. Many of these warm-ups lead to expanded stories and poems (see Figure 19).

The poem in Figure 19 was written by a second grade student. He began by listing the words *rainstorm, night, mansion, mom, dad,* and *sister* in his journal. Using his five senses, he then expanded his initial ideas into the poem.

Figure 19   **Storm in the Evening**

Looking out the window
into the pinkish sky . . .
weary halls behind me
and a fair wind blowing through
my hair . . . tiny lanterns all
through the room . . . the shiney
moon hanging over the shadowy
lake . . .
and mom sitting in her rocking
chair . . .
and Dad? and my sister? they were
in the mansion, too. And then,
just then, it happened . . . The
lightening struck, the thunder roared,
the rain poured on everything, even
on my hand hanging out of the
window . . . And then I realized, through
the rain I saw two dark mountains . . .
    by Danny

~Lesson 14

Literature Selection

Collect books featuring an About the Author page or jacket flap, one for each student.

Objectives

~ To use interviewing techniques

~ To create About the Author pages

Note: Prepare to spend several writers' workshop sessions to achieve Lesson 14 objectives. Once students have finished interviewing partners, have them use the organizational and management techniques from Lesson 7 to revise, edit, and complete the About the Author writing. Once work is completed, attach a photo of the author to the page, duplicate 5–10 copies, and store the copies in an oaktag pocket in the Authors' Corner (see Figure 20).

Vocabulary

~ interview

Getting Ready

Prepare a vocabulary strip.
Have available a sheet of 24-by-36-inch chart paper.

Step-by-Step Activities:

1. Invite students to join you at the Authors' Corner. Once students are gathered at the Authors' Corner, review objectives and vocabulary from previous lessons:

In a previous writers' workshop, we learned how authors use questions to expand topics and revise stories and how authors can use Question Strips to help them revise.

Does anyone remember what special words we use when we ask questions? (who, what, where, when, why, how)

2. Introduce new vocabulary:

Today we are going to learn facts about each other by conducting an interview.

Display the vocabulary strip:

What do you think the word interview *means?*

Accept all reasonable answers before defining the vocabulary word.

3. Select several books and read only the About the Author section to students. Suggestions for discussion:

What have we learned about the author? (List all the facts the students offer on a sheet of chart paper.)

What questions might have been asked of the author to get this information? (Refer to the facts listed on the chart and write a question for each fact.)

This question-and-answer technique is called an interview.

Is there any other information about this author that you'd like to know? (Answers will vary.)

Can you ask a question that would supply the answer? (List any new questions on the chart.)

What are some other questions we could ask in the interview? (Continue listing new questions on the chart.)

4. Prior to having students return to their work areas for writing time, say:

Today in your writing, interview a partner using the questions we listed as your guide. Answers you write down will be revised and edited and will become an About the Author section your partner can use for his or her published writing.

5. After the allotted time for writing, have students rejoin you at the Authors' Corner. Ask them to bring along any writing they would like to share with the group.

Use this lesson format to introduce Dedications, using books that contain dedications for the Literary selections.
(See also Part I, Chapter 2, "Writing, Revising, and Editing.")

Figure 20

```
┌─────────────────┐
│                 │
│                 │
│    (attach      │
│    student's    │
│    photo)       │
│                 │
│                 │
└─────────────────┘
```

About the Author Ryan

Ryan was born in East Setauket, N.Y. Ryan has published and illustrated 7 books. He goes to Nassakeag Elementary School, N.Y.

He collects little glass animals and baseball cards. His favorite technique is story-within-a-story. Ryan thinks each story he begins is his best until a new one is started.

~Lesson 15

Literature Selection

THE DAY JIMMY'S BOA ATE THE WASH
Trinka Hakes Noble
Illustrated by Steven Kellogg
New York: Dial Books, 1980

Summary

An ordinary class trip to a farm turns into a hilarious adventure.

Objective

~ To use quotation marks to introduce dialogue

Vocabulary

~ quotation marks

Getting Ready

Prepare a vocabulary strip.

Step-by-Step Activities

1. Invite students to join you at the Authors' Corner. Once students are gathered at the Authors' Corner, review objectives and vocabulary from previous lessons:

In our last two writers' workshops, we learned how authors use dialogue and interviews as writing techniques.

Does anyone remember what dialogue *and* interview *mean?*

2. Introduce new vocabulary:

Today we are going to learn how to use quotation marks *when writing dialogue.*

Display the vocabulary strips:

What do you think the words quotation marks *mean?*

Accept all reasonable answers before defining the vocabulary phrase.

3. Prior to reading *The Day Jimmy's Boa Ate the Wash,* ask:

Can anyone predict what the topic is?

Can anyone predict what characters we'll meet?

Can anyone predict where the story will take place? Can anyone predict the time of year? Can anyone predict the time of day?

4. Read the story to students. Suggestions for discussion:

What is the topic of the book? (a class trip to a farm)

Who are some of the characters we meet? (the girl narrator, her mother, the farmer, Jimmy, the boa, other classmates, the farmer's wife, Mrs. Stanley)

Where and when does the story take place? (on a farm in recent times)

How does Trinka Hakes Noble tell her story? (The narrator and her mother engage in a dialogue.)

How does the author show us that dialogue is used in her writing? (quotation marks)

Display several examples used by Trinka Hakes Noble in her book.

Authors use quotation marks in their writing to signal the use of dialogue. Quotation marks are placed before *the first word a character speaks and* after *the last word spoken.*

At this point, you may want to refer to the You Don't Say chart in the Authors' Corner before continuing the lesson (see Figure 1 and Lesson 3, Extended Activities).

5. Prior to having students return to their work areas for writing time, say:

Today in your writing, you may want to try using dialogue and quotation marks just as Trinka Hakes Noble did in The Day Jimmy's Boa Ate the Wash, *the book we have just finished reading.*

6. After the allotted time for writing, have students rejoin you at the Authors' Corner. Ask them to bring along any writing they would like to share with the group.

Related Bibliography

These books also support the lesson objective and could be used in place of *The Day Jimmy's Boa Ate the Wash*.

Cherry, Lynn. *The Great Kapok Tree.* New York: Harcourt Brace Jovanovich, 1990.

Halloran, Phyllis. "Colors Talk," a poem in *I'd Like To Hear the Flowers Grow.* Oregon City, Oregon: Reading, Inc., 1989.

Martin, Bill, Jr., and John Archambault. *Knots on a Counting Rope.* Illustrated by Ted Rand. New York: Holt, 1987.

Noble, Trinka Hakes. *Jimmy's Boa and the Big Splash Birthday Bash.* Illustrated by Steven Kellogg. New York: Dial Books for Young Readers, 1989.

Stolz, Mary. *Storm in the Night.* Illustrated by Pat Cummings. New York: Harper & Row, 1988.

Trompert, Ann. *Little Fox Goes to the End of the World.* Illustrated by John Wallner. New York: Crown Publishers, 1976.

Extended Activities

1. Create your own Mumbling Macaroni. Have your students cut pictures from magazines showing animals, humans, or inanimate characters. Distribute one piece of 9-by-12-inch construction paper to each student. Glue two of the characters on the construction paper, facing each other. Ask your students to imagine what the characters would be saying to each other and have them write the dialogue in their writing journals. Direct students' attention to the You Don't Say word bank in your Authors' Corner for ideas (see Figure 1 and Lesson 3). Help students revise and edit their writing before they copy the dialogue on the construction paper. Have students glue elbow macaroni quotation marks around the words the characters have spoken (see Figure 21).

Note: Students may use characters engaged in dialogue from their own writing for this activity. In that case, omit the magazine pictures and have students draw two characters before adding the dialogue and quotation marks.

2. Have students create their own Cartoon Capers. Copy as many Cartoon Caper sheets as you think you'll need (see page 79). Students can choose new topics and characters, or they can rewrite books they've already published, using a dialogue and cartoon format. Help students edit their dialogue before they publish their Cartoon Caper. When writing and artwork are completed, students cut strips apart, assemble the pages in the correct order, and staple them together as a Cartoon Caper.

Note: This activity can be used weekly to reinforce dialogue.

Figure 21

Cartoon Capers

Written and Illustrated by:

_____

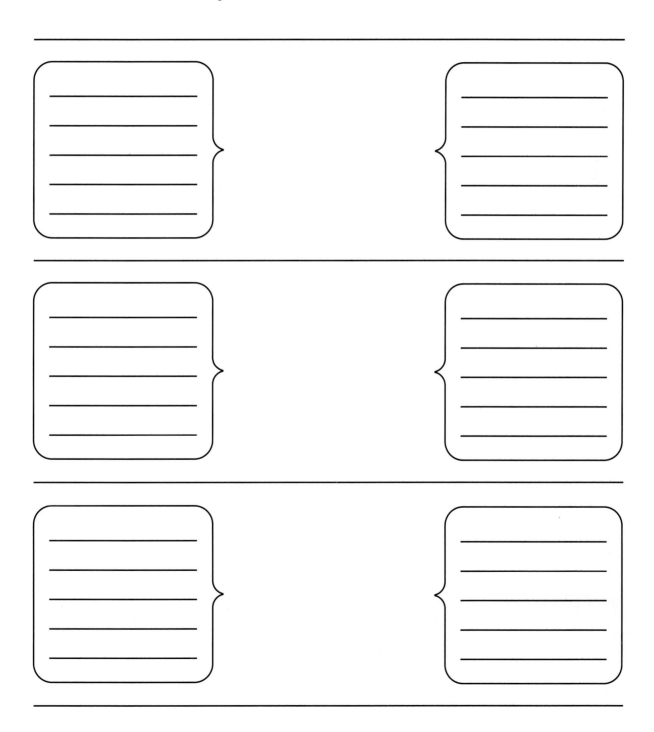

~Lesson 16

Literature Selection

MISS RUMPHIUS
Barbara Cooney
New York: Viking Press, 1982

Summary

Little Alice grows up, and along the way all her childhood wishes come true except for one. Now, as Miss Rumphius, Alice has one more promise to keep.

Objectives

~ To use the device of a narrator as a writing technique
~ To reinforce character and story development through the use of a narrator

Vocabulary

~ narrator

Getting Ready

Prepare a vocabulary strip.

Step-by-Step Activities

1. Invite students to join you at the Authors' Corner. Once students are gathered at the Authors' Corner, review objectives and vocabulary from the previous lesson by saying:

In our last writers' workshop, we learned how an author can use dialogue to tell a story.

Does anyone remember what dialogue *means?*

2. Introduce new vocabulary:

Today we are going to learn how authors use a narrator to tell a story.

Display the vocabulary strip:

What do you think this word means?

Accept all reasonable answers before defining the vocabulary word.

3. *Prior to reading* Miss Rumphius, *ask:*

Can anyone predict what the topic is?

Can anyone predict what characters we'll meet?

Can anyone predict where the story will take place? Can anyone predict the time of year? Can anyone predict the time of day?

4. Read the story to students. Suggestions for discussion:

What is the topic of the book? (Miss Rumphius's life)

Who are some of the characters we meet? (Miss Rumphius, her grandfather, Bapa Raja, and the narrator)

Where and when does the story take place? (in a village by the sea and places around the world; time shifts from long ago to present)

Who is telling the story? (Miss Rumphius's great-niece)

Often in stories, one person does the talking. Miss Rumphius's great-niece is called a narrator. *The story she is narrating is not about her. It is about her great-aunt. When authors have characters narrate their own stories, they use the word* I. *In* Miss Rumphius, *the great-niece uses the word* she *because the story is about someone other than herself.*

5. Prior to having students return to their work areas for writing time, say:

Today in your writing, you may want to try having a narrator tell a story just as Barbara Cooney did in Miss Rumphius, *the book we have just finished reading.*

6. After the allotted time for writing, have students rejoin you at the Authors' Corner. Ask them to bring along any writing they would like to share with the group.

Related Bibliography

These books also support the lesson objectives, and could be used in place of *Miss Rumphius.*

Bang, Molly. *The Paper Crane.* New York: Greenwillow, 1985.

Conrad, Pam. *The Tub People.* Illustrated by Richard Egielski. New York: Harper & Row, 1989.

Johnston, Tony, and Tomie de Paola. *The Quilt Story.* New York: Scholastic, 1985.

Smith, Buchanan Dozis. *The Taste of Blackberries.* New York: Harper & Row, 1988.

Williams, Vera. *A Chair for My Mother.* New York: Greenwillow Books, 1982.

Yolen, Jane. *Owl Moon.* New York: Philomel Books, 1987.

~Lesson 17

Literature Selection

A CHAIR FOR MY MOTHER
Vera Williams
New York: Greenwillow Books, 1982

Summary

When the big jar holding the coins is full, a little girl and her mother are going to buy a chair—the most beautiful, fat, soft arm chair in the world.

Objective

~ To reinforce story development through characterization (words and actions of characters)

Vocabulary

~ narration

Getting Ready

Prepare a vocabulary strip.

Step-by-Step Activities

1. Invite students to join you at the Authors' Corner. Once students are gathered at the Authors' Corner, review objectives and vocabulary from the previous lesson:

In our last writers' workshop, we saw how authors use narrators to tell a story.

Does anyone remember what narrator *means?*

Today we are going to see how another author uses narration *to write a story. Listen carefully to what her characters say and how they act toward each other.*

3. Prior to reading *A Chair for My Mother,* ask:

Can anyone predict what the topic is?

Can anyone predict what characters we'll meet?

Can anyone predict where the story will take place? Can anyone predict the time of year? Can anyone predict the time of day?

4. Read the story to students. Suggestions for discussion:

What is the topic of the book? (how a family saves money to buy a new chair)

Who are some of the characters we meet? (the little girl, her mother, and her grandmother)

Where and when does the story take place? (in the little girl's city neighborhood and apartment in recent times)

What kind of relationship do the little girl, her mother, and her grand-mother have? (warm, supportive, loving)

How does the author show us this? (through the characters' kind words and actions)

How does the author show us that the new chair made the characters happy and changed their lives? (through the illustrations and narration on the final pages)

5. Prior to having students return to their work areas for writing time, say:

Today in your writing, you may want to try narrating a story through characters' words and actions, just as Vera Williams did in A Chair for My Mother, *the book we have just finished reading.*

6. After the allotted time for writing, have students rejoin you at the Authors' Corner. Ask them to bring along any writing they would like to share with the group.

Related Bibliography

These books also support the lesson objectives and could be used in place of *A Chair for My Mother.*

de Paola, Tomie. *Now One Foot, Now Another.* New York: G.P. Putnam's Sons, 1984.

Hazen, Barbara Shook. *Tight Times.* Illustrated by Trina Schart Hyman. New York: Viking Press, 1979.

Isadore, Rachel. *Ben's Trumpet.* New York: Greenwillow Books, 1979.

MacLachlan, Patricia. *Through Grandpa's Eyes.* Illustrated by Deborah Kogan Ray. New York: Harper & Row, 1980.

Smith, Doris Buchanan. *A Taste of Blackberries.* New York: Harper & Row, 1988.

Trompert, Ann. *Little Fox Goes to the End of the World.* Illustrated by John Wallner. New York: Crown, 1976.

Waber, Bernard. *Ira Sleeps Over.* Boston: Houghton Mifflin, 1972.

~Lesson 18

Literature Selection

WHATEVER HAPPENED TO THE DINOSAURS?
Bernard Most
San Diego: Harcourt Brace Jovanovich, 1984

Summary

This book poses questions about dinosaurs, including where they went and why they became extinct. Scientists are not sure about the answers to these questions; students get to add their ideas.

Objectives

~ To use cause and effect to expand stories
~ To review Lesson 8 and Lesson 9 objectives (problem identification and solution)

Vocabulary

~ cause and effect

Getting Ready

Prepare vocabulary strips.
Prepare Basic Story Ingredients chart (see Figure 22).

Step-by-Step Activities

1. Invite students to join you at the Authors' Corner. Once students are gathered at the Authors' Corner, review objectives and vocabulary from previous lessons:

In previous writers' workshops, we have seen how important it is for an author to identify a problem and then solve it.

2. Introduce new vocabulary:

Today we are going to learn how an author uses cause and effect *to help audiences recognize and understand a story's problem and its solution.*

Display the vocabulary strip:

What do you think cause and effect *means?*

Accept all reasonable answers before defining the vocabulary phrase. Then say:

Today we will learn how authors use cause and effect to help their readers understand story problems and solutions.

Display the Basic Story Ingredients chart (see Figure 22).

3. Prior to reading *Whatever Happened to the Dinosaurs?*, ask:

Can anyone predict what the topic is?

Can anyone predict what characters we'll meet?

Can anyone predict where the story will take place? Can anyone predict the time of year? Can anyone predict the time of day?

4. Read the story to students. Suggestions for discussion:

What is the topic of the book? (the disappearance of all dinosaurs)

Who are some of the characters we meet? (many dinosaurs)

Where and when does the story take place? (imaginary settings)

Figure 22

Basic Story Ingredients

Beginning
    topic
    characters
    setting and time
    mood

Middle
    problem identified
      cause and effect

End
    problem solved
      cause and effect

What are some of the causes Bernard Most suggests? What effects would these causes have? (Answers will vary.)

Can anyone suggest other causes and effects that Bernard Most didn't mention? (Answers will vary.)

5. Prior to having students return to their work areas for writing time, say:

Today in your writing, you may want to try using cause and effect to help your audience understand the problem and solution in your story, just as Bernard Most did in Whatever Happened to the Dinosaurs?, *the book we have just finished reading.*

6. After the allotted time for writing, have students rejoin you at the Authors' Corner. Ask them to bring along any writing they would like to share with the group.

Related Bibliography

These books also support the lesson objectives and could be used in place of *Whatever Happened to the Dinosaurs?*

Barrett, Judi. *Animals Should Definitely Not Wear Clothing.* New York: Macmillan, 1989.

Bayley, Nicola. *Parrot Cat.* New York: Alfred A. Knopf, 1984.

See other Bayley titles, including *Polar Bear Cat, Spider Cat, Elephant Cat.* New York: Alfred A. Knopf, 1984.

Hutchins, Pat. *The Wind Blew.* New York: Puffin Books, 1974.

Most, Bernard. *If the Dinosaurs Came Back.* New York: Harcourt Brace Jovanovich, 1978.

Numeroff, Laura Joffe. *If You Give a Mouse a Cookie.* Illustrated by Felicia Bond. New York: Harper, 1985.

Turkle, Brinton. *Do Not Open.* New York: Dutton, 1981.

Extended Activity

Create your own Big Book of Dinosaurs. Distribute one piece of 9-by-12-inch drawing or construction paper to each student. Ask students to choose their favorite art medium and draw a scene that shows what might have happened to one of the dinosaurs. Have your students complete this phrase: Maybe all the dinosaurs _____. Help your students revise and edit their phrases before copying them on paper strips. Attach the strips to their artwork and publish as a book (see Figure 23).

Figure 23

~Lesson 19

Literature Selection

IF THE DINOSAURS CAME BACK
Bernard Most
San Diego: Harcourt Brace Jovanovich, 1978

Summary

This book poses a number of questions about dinosaurs, including where dinosaurs might reappear and how they might help us now. Students get a chance to add ideas of their own.

Objectives

~ To review Lesson 18 objectives
~ To use forecasting and prediction in writing

Vocabulary

~ forecast
~ predict

Getting Ready

Prepare vocabulary strips.
Have available the Basic Story Ingredients chart (see Figure 22).

Step-by-Step Activities

1. Invite students to join you at the Authors' Corner. Once students are gathered at the Authors' Corner, review objectives and vocabulary from the previous lesson:

In our last writers' workshop, we learned how authors use cause and effect to help audiences recognize and understand a story's problem and its solution.

Does anyone remember what cause and effect *means?*

2. Introduce new vocabulary:

Today we are going to learn how an author can forecast, *or* predict, *causes and effects.*

One at a time, display the vocabulary strips:

What do you think this word means?

Accept all reasonable answers before defining each vocabulary word.

3. Prior to reading *If the Dinosaurs Came Back,* ask:

Can anyone predict what the topic is?

Can anyone predict what characters we'll meet?

Can anyone predict where the story will take place? Can anyone predict the time of year? Can anyone predict the time of day?

4. Read the story to students. Suggestions for discussion:

What is the topic of the book? (predicting what would happen if dinosaurs returned)

Who are some of the characters we meet? (many dinosaurs)

Where and when does the story take place? (imaginary setting)

What were some of Bernard Most's predictions? Why would the dinosaurs be helpful for each of those jobs? (Answers will vary.)

Can anyone predict other ways in which dinosaurs could help us? Remember to think of cause and effect before you make predictions. (Answers will vary.)

Display Basic Story Ingredients chart (see Figure 22).

5. Prior to having students return to their work areas for writing time, say:

Today in your writing, you may want to try forecasting, just as Bernard Most did in If the Dinosaurs Came Back, *the book we have just finished reading.*

6. After the allotted time for writing, have students rejoin you at the Authors' Corner. Ask them to bring along any writing they would like to share with the group.

Related Bibliography

The following book and the books in the Lesson 18 Related Bibliography also support the lesson objectives and could be used in place of *If the Dinosaurs Came Back*.

Boynton, Sandra. *If at First*. Boston: Little, Brown, 1980.

Extended Activity

Follow directions for Lesson 18 Extended Activity, but have students predict how dinosaurs could be helpful if they returned (see Figure 24).

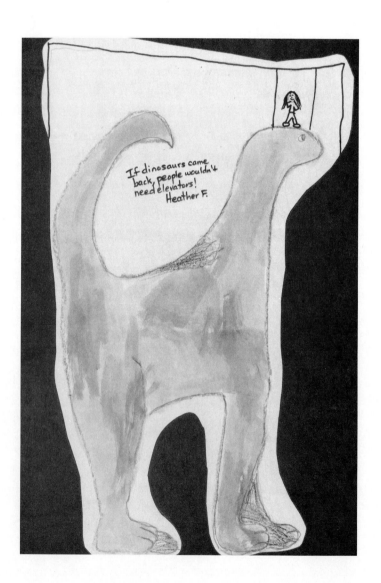

Figure 24

~Lesson 20

Literature Selection

IF YOU WERE A WRITER
Joan Lowery Nixon
Illustrated by Bruce Degen
New York: MacMillan, 1988

Summary

Melia's mother is a writer. Melia thinks she might like to be a writer, too. But what does a writer do?

Objectives

~ To recognize editing as a writer's responsibility

~ To use Publishing Sticks and the Editor's Checklist as a management technique (See Part I, Chapter 2, "Writing, Revising and Editing.")

Vocabulary

~ editing

~ Publishing Sticks

~ Editor's Checklist

Getting Ready

Prepare vocabulary strips.

Assemble the following materials:

~ markers

~ one library card pocket for each student, labeled with student's name (see Figure 3 and Figure 4)

~ one wooden tongue depressor for each student, labeled "I've Shared. I've Revised. I've Edited."

~ Editor's Checklist, prepared on 24-by-36-inch chart paper (see Figure 2 and Appendix)

Step-by-Step Activities:

1. Invite students to join you at the Authors' Corner. Once students are gathered at the Authors' Corner, review objectives and vocabulary from previous lessons:

In previous writers' workshops, we learned how writers develop ideas into stories.

Review vocabulary words from previous lessons as needed.

2. Introduce new vocabulary:

Today we are going to learn how an author edits a piece of writing.

One at a time, display vocabulary strips:

What do you think this word means?

Accept all reasonable answers before defining each vocabulary word.

3. Prior to reading *If You Were a Writer,* ask:

Can anyone predict what the topic is?

Can anyone predict what characters we'll meet?

Can anyone predict where the story will take place? Can anyone predict the time of year? Can anyone predict the time of day?

4. Read the story to students. Suggestions for discussion:

What is the topic of the book? (how to become a writer)

Who are some of the characters we meet? (Melia, her mother, her sisters, her uncle)

Where and when does the story take place? (at Melia's house in recent times)

What is some of the advice Melia's mother offers to help Melia become a writer? (Use words that paint pictures; Show, don't tell; Writers get ideas everywhere; Ideas are just a beginning; Create exciting settings for your characters; Words such as "What if . . ." help identify and solve story problems.)

Where did Melia's mother send her writing to be turned into books? (a publishing company, where it was edited again before being published)

Introduce Editor's Checklist responsibilities and use of Publishing Sticks at this time (see Figures 2, 3, and 4; Part I: "Writing, Revising, and Editing"; Appendix).

5. Prior to having students return to their work areas for writing time, say:

Today in your writing, you may want to try editing a piece of writing that is ready to be published. Use the Editor's Checklist and Publishing Sticks to help you.

6. After the allotted time for writing, have students rejoin you at the Authors' Corner. Ask them to bring along any writing they would like to share with the group.

Related Bibliography

This book also supports the lesson objectives and could be used in place of *If You Were a Writer.*

Aliki. *How a Book Is Made.* New York: Thomas Crowell, 1986.

~Lesson 21

Literature Selection

A House Is a House for Me
Mary Ann Hoberman
Illustrated by Betty Fraser
New York: Viking Press, 1978

Summary

Through rhymes, Mary Ann Hoberman catalogues the dwellings of various animals and things in our world.

Objective

~ To use repetition as a writing technique

Vocabulary

~ repetition
~ technique

Getting Ready

Prepare vocabulary strips.

Step-by-Step Activities

1. Invite students to join you at the Authors' Corner. Once students are gathered at the Authors' Corner, review objectives and vocabulary from the previous lessons:

In our last writers' workshop, we saw how authors edit their writing.

Review vocabulary words from previous lessons as needed.

2. Introduce new vocabulary:

Today we are going to learn how authors can use specific techniques when they write.

One at a time, display vocabulary strips:

What do you think this word means?

Accept all reasonable answers before defining each vocabulary word.

3. Prior to reading *A House Is a House for Me*, ask:

Can anyone predict what the topic is?

Can anyone predict what characters we'll meet?

Can anyone predict where the story will take place? Can anyone predict the time of year? Can anyone predict the time of day?

4. Read the story to students. Suggestions for discussion:

What is the topic of the book? (houses for various animals and things)

Who are some of the characters we meet? (many animals, children)

Did the author repeat any words throughout the story? ("A house is a house for me. . . .")

This technique is called repetition. *Sometimes authors use these word patterns as a specific* technique *in their writing.*

5. Prior to having students return to their work areas for writing time, say:

Today in your writing, you may want to try using repetition as a technique, just as Mary Ann Hoberman did in A House Is a House for Me, *the book we have just finished reading.*

6. After the allotted time for writing, have students rejoin you at the Authors' Corner. Ask them to bring along any writing they would like to share with the group.

Related Bibliography

These books also support the lesson objective and could be used in place of *A House Is a House for Me.*

Hutchins, Pat. *Good Night Owl.* New York: Macmillan, 1972.

Serfozo, Mary. *Who Said Red?* Illustrated by Keiko Narahashi. New York: Scholastic, 1988.

Slobodkina, Esphyr. *Caps For Sale*. New York: Harper & Row, 1947.

Sutton, Eve. *My Cat Likes To Hide in Boxes*. Illustrated by Lynley Dodd. New York: Viking Penguin Books, 1973.

Wood, Audrey. *Quick As a Cricket*. Illustrated by Don Wood. Sudbury, Mass.: Childs Play International Ltd., 1982.

Extended Activity

Create your own "A House Is a House" class book. Ask students to think of many varied and unusual dwellings for animals and/or things Mary Ann Hoberman *hasn't* mentioned. Students can choose their favorite art media (crayons, markers, tempera paints, watercolors) and illustrate their idea. Ask several students to do an illustration of their *own* house as well. Add the repetitive phrase "But a house is a house for me!" to these illustrations. When collating the artwork and writing, insert the extra illustrations every 2–4 pages, following Mary Ann Hoberman's pattern.

~Lesson 22

Literature Selection

GOOD NIGHT OWL
Pat Hutchins
New York: MacMillan, 1972

Summary

Poor owl tries to sleep through the daytime noises that surround him.

Objective

~ To use surprise as a writing technique

Vocabulary

~ element of surprise

Getting Ready

Prepare a vocabulary strip.

Step-by-Step Activities

1. Invite students to join you at the Authors' Corner. Once students are gathered at the Authors' Corner, review objectives and vocabulary from the previous lesson:

In our last writers' workshop, we learned how authors use repetition as a writing technique.

Does anyone remember what repetition *and* technique *mean?*

2. Introduce new vocabulary:

Today we are going to learn how authors use the element of surprise *as a writing technique.*

Display the vocabulary strip.

What do you think the words element of surprise *mean?*

Accept all reasonable answers before defining the vocabulary phrase.

3. Prior to reading *Good Night Owl,* ask:

Can anyone predict what the topic is?

Can anyone predict what characters we'll meet?

Can anyone predict where the story will take place? Can anyone predict the time of year? Can anyone predict the time of day?

4. Read the story to students. Suggestions for discussion:

What is the topic of the book? (Owl tries to sleep.)

Who are some of the characters we meet? (Owl, woodland creatures)

Where and when does the story take place? (in a forest; daytime into night)

Did anyone notice the use of repetition? ("Owl tried to sleep.")

How was the last page different? (The author surprised us: The owl screeched and woke everyone up.)

This technique is called the element of surprise. *Authors sometimes use the element of surprise along with repetition. This technique helps authors to avoid boring repetition and usually makes the reader or listener laugh in surprise.*

5. Prior to having students return to their work areas for writing time, say:

Today in your writing, you may want to try using an element of surprise as a writing technique just as Pat Hutchins did in Good Night Owl, *the book we have just finished reading.*

6. After the allotted time for writing, have students rejoin you at the Authors' Corner. Ask them to bring along any writing they would like to share with the group.

Related Bibliography

These books also support the lesson objectives and could be used in place of *Good Night Owl*.

Gag, Wanda. *Millions of Cats.* New York: Scholastic, 1956.

Hoberman, Mary Ann. *A House Is a House for Me.* Illustrated by Betty Fraser. New York: Viking, 1978.

Lindberg, Reeve. *The Day the Goose Got Loose.* New York: Doubleday, 1990.

Mahy, Margaret. *The Boy Who Was Followed Home.* Illustrated by Steven Kellogg. New York: Dial, 1986.

Van Allsburg, Chris. *Just a Dream.* Boston: Houghton Mifflin, 1990.

Waber, Bernard. *Just Like Abraham Lincoln.* Boston: Houghton Mifflin, 1964.

~Lesson 23

Literature Selection

QUICK AS A CRICKET
Audrey Wood
Illustrated by Don Wood
Sudbury, Mass.: Child's Play International Ltd., 1982

Summary

People and animals are alike.

Objectives

~ To use comparison and simile as a writing technique
~ To use *like* and *as* in forming comparisons and similes

Vocabulary

~ comparison
~ simile

Getting Ready

Prepare vocabulary strips.

Step-by-Step Activities

1. Invite students to join you at the Authors' Corner. Once students are gathered at the Authors' Corner, review objectives and vocabulary from the previous lessons:

In our last few writers' workshops, we learned how authors use specific writing techniques.

Does anyone remember any of the techniques we've seen? (repetition, element of surprise)

2. Introduce new vocabulary:

Today we are going to learn how authors use comparison *and* simile *as writing techniques.*

One at a time, display vocabulary strips:

What do you think this word means?

Accept all reasonable answers before defining each vocabulary word.

3. Prior to reading *Quick as a Cricket,* ask:

Can anyone predict what the topic is?

Can anyone predict what characters we'll meet?

Can anyone predict where the story will take place? Can anyone predict the time of year? Can anyone predict the time of day?

4. Read the story to students. Suggestions for discussion:

What is the topic of the book? (A child compares himself to animals.)

Who are some of the characters we meet? (the girl, a cricket, a bunny, an ox, and so on)

How does the author show how strong, mean, big, and cold the little boy is? (by comparing the traits of humans to animals most closely associated with that trait)

What word does the author use in each comparison? (as)

Authors use as *or* like *when they compare things. This comparison is called a* simile.

5. Prior to having students return to their work areas for writing time, say:

Today in your writing, you may want to try using comparisons and similes to make your ideas more specific, just as Audrey Wood did in Quick as a Cricket, *the book we have just finished reading.*

6. After the allotted time for writing, have students rejoin you at the Authors' Corner. Ask them to bring along any writing they would like to share with the group.

Related Bibliography

These books also support the lesson objectives and could be used in place of *Quick as a Cricket*.

Crew, Donald. *Blue Sea*. New York: Greenwillow, 1979.

Hoban, Tana. *Is It Larger? Is It Smaller?*. New York: Greenwillow, 1985.

Kellogg, Steven. *Much Bigger Than a Martin*. New York: Dutton, 1976.

Laurencin, Genevieve. *I Wish I Were*. Illustrated by Ulises Wensell. New York: Putnam, 1987.

Lionni, Leo. *The Biggest House in the World*. New York: Pantheon, 1968.

Schwartz, David. *How Much Is a Million?* New York: Scholastic, 1985.

Shaw, Charles. *It Looked Like Spilt Milk*. New York: Scholastic, 1989.

Titherington, Jeanne. *Big World, Small World*. New York: Greenwillow, 1985.

Zolotow, Charlotte. *Summer Is.* Illustrated by Ruth Lercher Bornstein. New York: Crowell, 1983.

Extended Activities

1. Have children use *bigger* and *smaller* as a basis of comparison for objects in our world.

For example: A puddle is like a lake, only smaller.

A mountain is like an anthill, only bigger.

A collection of these comparisons could be published as a list poem.

2. Take your class on a walk outdoors. Have them bring their writing materials. Ask them to look for and complete comparisons you've listed on a chart. Use ideas such as the following:

as rough as

as smooth as

as green as

as furry as

You might want to introduce *metaphors* in the same way. Some examples include a carpet of grass, a blanket of snow, and a tower of strength.

~Lesson 24

Literature Selection

WHERE THE WILD THINGS ARE
Maurice Sendak
New York: Harper & Row, 1988

Summary

Max is sent to his room without dinner and embarks on a wonderful adventure.

Objectives

~ To use a story-within-a-story as a writing technique

~ To use dream sequences to create a story-within-a-story

~ To use the idea of flashback to create a story-within-a-story (optional)

Vocabulary

~ story-within-a-story

Getting Ready

Prepare a vocabulary strip.

Step-by-Step Activities

1. Invite students to join you at the Authors' Corner. Once students are gathered at the Authors' Corner, review objectives and vocabulary from previous lessons:

In our last few writers' workshops, we learned how authors use different writing techniques.

Does anyone remember any of the techniques we've discussed? (repetition, element of surprise, comparison, simile)

2. Introduce new vocabulary:

Today we are going to learn how authors use dreams to create a story-within-a-story.

Display the vocabulary strip:

What do you think the words story-within-a-story *mean?*

Accept all reasonable answers before defining the vocabulary phrase.

3. Prior to reading *Where the Wild Things Are,* ask:

Can anyone predict what the topic is?

Can anyone predict what characters we'll meet?

Can anyone predict where the story will take place? Can anyone predict the time of year? Can anyone predict the time of day?

4. Read the story to students. Suggestions for discussion:

What is the topic of the book? (Max is sent to bed without supper.)

Is there another story told? (Max's dream)

What is the topic of this other story? (a trip to where the wild things live)

This technique is called a story-within-a-story.

What characters do we meet in the story-within-a-story? (Max, the wild things)

Where does the story-within-a-story take place? (in an imaginary land)

Where does the first story take place? (in Max's house)

How does the author enable the story-within-a-story to be told? (Max is sent to bed where he either dreams or imagines the story.)

One easy way for authors to use story-within-a-story is to have characters fall asleep and dream.

5. Prior to having students return to their work areas for writing time, say:

Today in your writing, you may want to try having your characters recall or dream a story-within-a-story, just as Maurice Sendak did in Where the Wild Things Are, *the book we have just finished reading.*

6. After the allotted time for writing, have students rejoin you at the Authors' Corner. Ask them to bring along any writing they would like to share with the group.

Related Bibliography

These books also support the lesson objectives and could be used in place of *Where the Wild Things Are*.

Browne, Anthony. *The Gorilla*. New York: A. Knopf, 1985.

Joyce, William. *George Shrinks*. New York: Harper & Row, 1985.

Tejima. *Fox's Dream*. New York: Scholastic, 1992.

Van Allsburg, Chris. *Jumanji*. Boston: Houghton Mifflin, 1981.

———. *Ben's Dream*. Boston: Houghton Mifflin, 1982.

———. *Polar Express*. Boston: Houghton Mifflin, 1985.

———. *Just a Dream*. Boston: Houghton Mifflin, 1990.

Extended Activity

Create a class book titled *Wild Things*. Have each student use her or his favorite art medium to make a wild thing. Students can then use adjectives and gerunds to describe their wild things, just as they did for the animals in Lesson 3.

For example:

Terrifying / Scary / Ugly / Horned / Wild thing!

Note: Tissue paper collage works well for this project (see Figure 25).

Figure 25

Gorgo....
Scaly, spiny
Stalking, threatening, pouncing
Always wary; ever observant
Monster!   by Jahbrele

~Lesson 25

THAT NEW PET
Alane Ferguson
Illustrated by Catherine Stock
New York: Lothrop, Lee & Shepard, 1986

Summary

When a new baby arrives in one family's household, the pets are not very happy!

Objectives

~ To use personification as a writing technique
~ To review dialogue and use of quotation marks (see Lessons 12, 13, and 15)

Vocabulary

~ personification

Getting Ready

Prepare a vocabulary strip.

Step-by-Step Activities

1. Invite students to join you at the Authors' Corner. Once students are gathered at the Authors' Corner, review objectives and vocabulary from previous lessons:

In our previous writers' workshops, we learned how authors use different writing techniques.

Does anyone remember the techniques we've discussed? (repetition, element of surprise, comparisons, similes, story-within-a-story)

2. Introduce new vocabulary:

Today we are going to learn how authors use personification *in their writing.*

Display the vocabulary strip:

What do you think the word personification *means?*

Accept all reasonable answers before defining the vocabulary word.

3. Prior to reading *That New Pet,* ask:

Can anyone predict what the topic is?

Can anyone predict what characters we'll meet?

Can anyone predict where the story will take place? Can anyone predict the time of year? Can anyone predict the time of day?

4. Read the story to students. Suggestions for discussion:

What is the topic of the book? (how Siam feels about the new baby)

Who are some of the characters we meet? (Crackers, Bones, Joanie, Teddy, the new baby, Siam)

Where and when does the story take place? (in Joan and Teddy's house, recent times)

Who is telling the story? (Siam, the cat)

Can animals really speak? (no)

Having a nonhuman character use words to communicate is called personification.

5. Prior to having students return to their work areas for writing time, say:

Today in your writing, you may want to try using personification, just as Alane Ferguson did in That New Pet, *the book we have just finished reading.*

6. After the allotted time for writing, have students rejoin you at the Authors' Corner. Ask them to bring along any writing they would like to share with the group.

These books also support the lesson objectives and could be used in place of *That New Pet.*

Note: Any book in which you find animals or inanimate objects speaking can be used to meet the objectives of this lesson.

Cherry, Lynn. *The Great Kapok Tree.* New York: Harcourt Brace Jovanovich, 1990.

Lawson, Robert. *Rabbit Hill.* New York: Puffin Books, 1972.

Minarik, Else Holmelund. *Little Bear.* Illustrated by Maurice Sendak. New York: Harper & Row, 1957.

Trompert, Anne. *Little Fox Goes to the End of the World.* Illustrated by John Wallner. New York: Crown, 1976.

~Lesson 26

Literature Selection

TWO BAD ANTS
Chris Van Allsburg
Boston: Houghton Mifflin, 1988

Summary

Two greedy ants venture into a kitchen and the dangerous arena of breakfast preparation.

Objective

~ To use point of view as a writing technique

(*Note:* The artwork in this book also provides an excellent example of visual point of view.)

Vocabulary

~ point of view

Getting Ready

Prepare a vocabulary strip.

Step-by-Step Activities

1. Invite students to join you at the Authors' Corner. Once students are gathered at the Authors' Corner, review objectives and vocabulary from previous lessons:

In our last few writers' workshops, we learned how authors use different writing techniques.

Does anyone remember any of the techniques we've discussed? (repetition, element of surprise, comparisons, similes, story-within-a-story, personification)

2. Introduce new vocabulary:

Today we are going to learn how authors can use point of view *in their writing.*

Display the vocabulary strip:

What do you think the words point of view *mean?*

Accept all reasonable answers before defining the vocabulary word.

3. Prior to reading *Two Bad Ants,* ask:

Can anyone predict what the topic is?

Can anyone predict what characters we'll meet?

Can anyone predict where the story will take place? Can anyone predict the time of year? Can anyone predict the time of day?

4. Read the story to students. Suggestions for discussion:

What is the topic of the book? (the adventures of two ants)

Who are some of the characters we meet? (ants)

Where and when does the story take place? (in the ants' natural habitat as well as in a kitchen)

Who is telling the story? (an unnamed narrator)

Whose story is being told? (the ants' story)

Seeing things as the character sees them is called point of view. *In this book, we experience the world of nature as well as an ordinary kitchen through the eyes of a tiny insect.*

What words does the author use to help us understand that the story is being told from the ants' point of view? (a brick wall becomes a "mountain"; a crack in the wall becomes a "tunnel"; a teaspoon becomes "a giant silver scoop")

How do the illustrations help us understand the ants' point of view? (They, too, give us a different perspective.)

5. Prior to having students return to their work areas for writing time, say:

Today in your writing, you may want to try telling a story from a particular point of view, just as Chris Van Allsburg did in Two Bad Ants, *the book we have just finished reading.*

6. After the allotted time for writing, have students rejoin you at the Authors' Corner. Ask them to bring along any writing they would like to share with the group.

Related Bibliography

These books also support the lesson objective and could be used in place of *Two Bad Ants.*

Bayley, Nicola. *Parrot Cat.* New York: A. Knopf, 1984.

Blaine, Marge. *The Terrible Thing That Happened At Our House.* Illustrated by John C. Wallner. New York: Parent's Magazine Press, 1975.

Blume, Judy. *The Pain and The Great One.* Illustrated by Irene Trivas. New York: Dell, 1974.

Browne, Anthony. *Piggybook.* New York: A. Knopf, 1986.

Munsch, Robert N. *The Paper Bag Princess.* Toronto: Annick Press Ltd., 1980.

Ryder, Joanne. *Chipmunk Song.* Illustrated by Lynne Cherry. New York: Dutton, 1987.

———. *The Snail's Spell.* Illustrated by Lynne Cherry. New York; Puffin Books, 1988.

Scieszka, Jon. *The Frog Prince Continued.* Illustrated by Steve Johnson. New York: Viking, 1991.

———, and A. Wolf. *The True Story of the Three Little Pigs.* Illustrated by Lane Smith. New York: Viking, 1989.

Titherington, Jeanne. *Big World, Small World.* New York: Greenwillow, 1985.

Viorst, Judith. *Alexander and the Terrible, Horrible, No Good, Very Bad Day.* Illustrated by Ray Cruz. New York: Macmillan, 1972.

———. *I'll Fix Anthony.* New York: Atheneum, 1969.

———. *Rosie and Michael.* Illustrated by Lorna Tomei. New York: Atheneum, 1974.

Wolff, Ashley. *Only the Cat Saw.* New York: Dodd, Mead and Company, 1985.

Extended Activities

1. Children can think of other creatures in our world (or imaginary ones, such as giants) and create drawings of real-life environments as seen from the creature's point of view.

2. Fairy tales, fables, and folk tales all offer a perfect opportunity for retelling from a different point of view. Two excellent sources are *The True Story of the Three Little Pigs,* by A. Wolf as told to Jon Scieszka, and *The Paper Bag Princess* by Robert Munsch (see Related Bibliography).

3. Discuss basic story ingredients for specific genres:

~ fairy tales—use of the numbers 3, 7, 9, 12; the hero is usually royalty; the heroine is usually down-trodden but beautiful; the villain is sometimes a monster, there is a predictably happy ending

~ fables—lesson taught

~ folk tales—repetition of plot and characters

~ tall tales—exaggeration

Invite students to create a modern fairy tale, folk tale, fable, or tall tale, telling it from a specific point of view.

4. Have your students make Naughty Picnic Ants (see Figure 26). This project can be used as a story starter.

Figure 26
Naughty Picnic Ants

To make the ants, have students trace three circles on black or brown construction paper, cut out circles, and attach them together using brass paper fasteners. Pipe cleaners may be used to create legs and antennae. When a small magnet is held under the plate, the ants appear to be scurrying around eating the food.

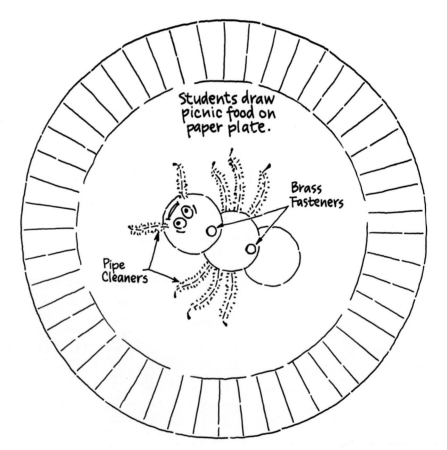

Students draw picnic food on paper plate.

Brass Fasteners

Pipe Cleaners

~Lesson 27

Literature Selection

THE WIND BLEW
Pat Hutchins
New York: Macmillan, 1986

Summary

A wind blows into town and creates havoc before finally blowing
out to sea.

Objective

~ To use foreshadowing as a writing and illustrative technique

Note: Foreshadowing as a writing technique is best introduced to
intermediate students. (See Related Bibliography for two literature
selections.) Primary students, however, can best understand foreshadowing as a technique through art.

Vocabulary

~ foreshadow

Getting Ready

Prepare a vocabulary strip.

Step-by-Step Activities

1. Invite students to join you at the Authors' Corner. Once students are gathered at the Authors' Corner, review objectives and
vocabulary from previous lessons:

In our last few writers' workshops, we learned how authors use different writing techniques.

Does anyone remember any of the techniques we've discussed? (repetition, element of surprise, comparisons, similes, story-within-a-story, personification, point of view)

2. Introduce new vocabulary:

Today we are going to learn how authors and artists can foreshadow *what is going to happen in their writing.*

Display the vocabulary strip:

What do you think the word foreshadow *means?*

Accept all reasonable answers before defining the vocabulary word.

3. Prior to reading *The Wind Blew,* ask:

Can anyone predict what the topic is?

Can anyone predict what characters we'll meet?

Can anyone predict where the story will take place? Can anyone predict the time of year? Can anyone predict the time of day?

4. Read the story to students. Suggestions for discussion:

What is the topic of the book? (the wind blowing through a town)

Who are some of the characters we meet? (the judge, the twins, and other townspeople)

Where and when does the story take place? (in any town in recent times)

Look carefully at the page again. How has Pat Hutchins used artwork to give her audience clues about what will happen next? (The little girl's balloon will fly away on the next page.)

Pat Hutchins uses artwork to predict what will happen next, which is expressed in words. This technique is called foreshadowing. *Just as weather forecasters predict what will happen to our weather, authors and artists can use foreshadowing in words and pictures to tell what will happen next in their stories.*

Continue with the rest of the book, citing how artwork *foreshadows* action.

5. Prior to having students return to their work areas for writing time, say:

Today in your writing, you may want to try to foreshadow what will happen next, just as Pat Hutchins did in The Wind Blew, *the book we have just finished reading.*

6. After the allotted time for writing, have students rejoin you at the Authors' Corner. Ask them to bring along any writing they would like to share with the group.

Related Bibliography

These books also support the lesson objective and could be used in place of *The Wind Blew.*

Base, Graeme. *The 11th Hour.* New York: Harry N. Abrams, 1989.

Brett, Jan. *Annie and the Wild Animals.* Boston: Houghton Mifflin, 1985.

————. *The Mitten.* New York: G.P. Putnam and Sons, 1989.

For older students, reinforce foreshadowing as a writing technique using these books:

Lewis, C.S. *The Lion, the Witch and the Wardrobe.* New York: Macmillan, 1988.

Smith, Doris B. *The Taste of Blackberries.* New York: Harper & Row, 1973.

(Both books use a change of weather to foreshadow events to come.)

Extended Activity

After reading *The Wind Blew,* by Pat Hutchins, have students imagine themselves in similar circumstances: They are in their own setting when a terrible wind blows through. Ask students to place themselves in that setting and list all of the many varied and unusual things that could happen. After listing these happenings, ask them to draw a profile of themselves reacting to this momentous wind, showing how, artistically speaking, their hair stands on end (see Figure 27).

Students can also create list poems that can then be revised, edited, and published as accompanying text to their artwork.

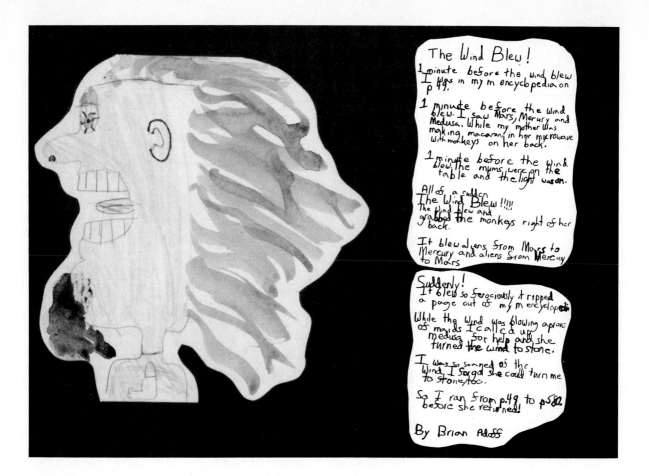

Figure 27

~Lesson 28

Literature Selection

ASTER AARDVARK'S ALPHABET ADVENTURES
Steven Kellogg
New York: Morrow Junior Books, 1987

Summary

Steven Kellogg shares his wonderful, witty, wacky way with words.

Objective

~ To use alliteration as a writing technique

Vocabulary

~ alliteration

Getting Ready

Prepare a vocabulary strip.

Step-by-Step Activities

1. Invite students to join you at the Authors' Corner. Once students are gathered at the Authors' Corner, review objectives and vocabulary from previous lessons:

In our last few writers' workshops, we learned how authors use different writing techniques.

Does anyone remember any of the techniques we've discussed?
(repetition, element of surprise, comparisons, similes, story-within-a-story, personification, point of view, foreshadowing)

2. Introduce new vocabulary:

Today we are going to learn how authors and artists use alliteration *in their writing.*

Display the vocabulary strip:

What do you think the word alliteration *means?*

Accept all reasonable answers before defining the vocabulary word.

3. Prior to reading *Aster Aardvark's Alphabet Adventures*, ask:

Can anyone predict what the topic is?

Can anyone predict what characters we'll meet?

Does anyone recognize anything special about the title? (All the words begin with the letter "A," an alliteration.)

Can anyone predict where the story will take place? Can anyone predict the time of year? Can anyone predict the time of day?

4. Read the story to students. Suggestions for discussion:

What is the topic of the book? (Aster's adventures)

Who are some of the characters we meet? (many different animals)

Where and when does the story take place? (many different locations)

Did anyone notice how the author uses alliteration? (Each creature's name and actions begin with the same letter.)

5. Prior to having students return to their work areas for writing time, say:

Today in your writing, you may want to try alliteration, just as Steven Kellogg did in Aster Aardvark's Alphabet Adventures, *the book we have just finished reading.*

6. After the allotted time for writing, have students rejoin you at the Authors' Corner. Ask them to bring along any writing they would like to share with the group.

Related Bibliography

Note: Many authors use alliterative writing sparingly in their texts to achieve specific purposes. Be on the lookout for examples you can share with your class. Steven Kellogg's book is an atypical example of the use of alliteration but works well as an introduction to this writing technique. You may want to consider using other ABC books to introduce alliteration, inviting your students to expand upon the idea.

These books also support the lesson objectives and could be used in place of *Aster Aardvark's Alphabet Adventures.*

Base, Graeme. *Animalia.* New York: Abrams, 1987.

Geisert, Arthur. *Pigs from A to Z.* Boston: Houghton Mifflin, 1986.

Levinson, Riki. *I Go with My Family to Grandma's.* Illustrated by Diane Goode. New York: Bantam Doubleday Dell Publishing Group, 1990.

Neumeir, Marty, and Byron Glaser. *Action Alphabet.* New York: Greenwillow, 1984.

Extended Activity

Create your own Creative Critters class book. Have your students write the name of their creatures using alliteration. Crispy Crawler is an example. Have your students write what it eats, some of its favorite activities, how it protects itself, and one really bad thing it has done. Use alliteration for each item (see Figure 28). Distribute one piece of 9-by-12-inch light-colored construction paper to each student and have him or her choose a favorite art medium to make a Creative Critter. Help your students revise and edit their writing before copying it on strips of paper. Attach the strips to the artwork and publish it as a book.

Figure 28

My creature's name is Taffy
It lives in Ticher on the top of
a tower.
She eats tangerines, trees
and drinks tea.
She likes to play with tape
and she likes to type.
She likes to play with termites
and play tag, also.
She has lots of talent
And when I met her she tickled
my toes.

by Amanda

IV ~Appendix

~How to Start an In-School Publishing Company

The dream of establishing an in-house publishing company is about to come true. This is a very exciting prospect, but be prepared. The many hours and days of hard work ahead will seem endless and tiresome, but there will be tremendous rewards. You will have had a part in putting authors' work into the hand of readers! GOOD LUCK!

Weeks 1 and 2

1. Choose two people among your 15–20 organizers who will be in charge of at-home volunteers who have access to sewing machines and in-school volunteers who are comfortable using bindery machinery.

2. Contact a school equipment company to order bindery machines (see page 130), and set up a training session with a company representative. Have two parents and two teachers at this session.

3. Promote the publishing company opening by having an art teacher design a logo. You may wish to put the logo on buttons. Post hall notices and circulate information to teachers and families. Hold a faculty meeting to explain the project.

4. Prepare and send a survey and/or letter home to all families via classroom teachers. Set up a box for returned responses in the main office and have two people collect and collate returns.

5. Set dates for training sessions (we suggest four training sessions: one during school hours, one during the afternoon, and two during the evening); apply for building use; arrange for coffee and cookies for all sessions; and gather any necessary materials.

Nassakeag School Publishing Company

NAME —————————————————————————

CLASS —————————————————————————

PHONE —————————————————————————

1. Please check either box or both boxes:

   I can work at home.   ❏

   I can work in school.   ❏

   Days of the week I am available: M   T   W   Th   F

   Hours I am available: morning   afternoon   evening

2. I can donate fabric scraps.   ❏

   I have access to a sewing machine.   ❏

   I can donate wallpaper samples.   ❏

   I have other materials that can   ❏
   be used. (List them below.)

   ——————————————————————————

   ——————————————————————————

   ——————————————————————————

   ——————————————————————————

   ——————————————————————————

Dear Nassakeag Families,

The NASSAKEAG SCHOOL PUBLISHING COMPANY is in the process of setting up shop, and we are looking for people to make cloth- and wallpaper-covered bound books (called signatures).

Making signatures involves simply sewing a seam down the center of several pieces of paper (if you do not have access to a sewing machine, one could be provided) and then making a cover for them with fabric or wallpaper.

If you feel that you would be able to help with this simple process either at school or at home, please return the tear-off sheet below to Joanne Graham, Nassakeag School Publishing Company, at the main office.

We also need a supply of fabric, wallpaper, and cardboard. Should you have any of these items gathering dust, please send them into the Publishing Room so that we can continue to make signatures for our growing list of Nassakeag authors.

If there is someone out there who would enjoy transcribing a child's written work into a published book, please let us know who you are.

Please return the sheet below as soon as possible so that our authors can get on with the excitement of publishing a book of their own.

Thank you.

. . . .

❏ I will sew.

❏ I will sew and make covers.

❏ I have material.

❏ I have wallpaper.

❏ I have cardboard.

❏ I will transcribe a child's
    work into a book.

NAME _____

TELEPHONE _____

CHILD'S TEACHER _____

Weeks 3–4

1. Notify parents and teachers of training workshop dates and have responses returned to a box in the main office. *Be sure to recruit teachers for these workshops!*

2. Choose a room within the building that is able to house machines and supplies for the publishing company.

3. Have volunteers gather supplies and inventory them in the publishing company room. Some necessary items are listed below.

~ blank ditto paper

~ large and small signature sheets

~ cardboard

~ wallpaper and fabric

~ filmstrip materials (pens, blank filmstrip rolls, canisters)

~ glue sticks

~ glue that won't bleed through fabric or paper

~ white liquid glue

~ scissors

~ rulers

~ pens

~ clear contact paper

~ stapler

~ manila folders

~ two boxes (labeled "To Be Published" and "Published") for machine publishing

~ machine supplies (laminate, binders)

~ blank books

~ one box for completed blank books

~ monthly calendar for in-school volunteer sign-up for next session

The Grand Opening

Set a date and make the Grand Opening a celebration! Publish one of each kind of book you are producing: spiral bound, flat bound, fabric covered, and wallpaper covered. Display them with a balloon bouquet in the main office. The response will be fantastic!

On the same day:

1. Distribute publishing company rules and regulations packets to teachers and post a copy in the publishing company and on the bulletin board in the teachers' lounge.

2. Distribute and post the volunteer schedule for the first month.

3. As materials become available, let teachers know.

4. At this time, teachers who have been trained may want to send home invitations to their students' parents for future training sessions, thus ensuring a constant new pool of publishers.

CONGRATULATIONS!
YOU'RE ON YOUR WAY!

Toot Your Own Horn

Now that you have successfully put writers into the hands of readers, let everyone know!

One of the easiest ways is to designate one of your volunteers to be a public relations liaison. Don't forget:

1. Have your principal set aside time each week for newly published authors to come and share their published work (principals can hand out special awards).

2. Select an Author and Artist of the Month and publicize their accomplishments.

3. Make check-out cards for each Author and Artist of the Month winner and have a duplicate book published so that the school library can display it and circulate it.

4. Make photocopies of other books for display in the library and main office.

5. Contact your local community library about the possibility of displaying students' writing.

Finally, thank all who have helped!

Each year, we hold two separate receptions, one to thank volunteers for their time and another to celebrate individual classroom authors' accomplishments. These receptions are held in June after school hours. Student artists are chosen to create the invitation cover design, and refreshments are served. Small gifts or certificates may be given to volunteers. The "Celebration of Writing" evening is held on a strictly volunteer basis; only those teachers willing to participate are asked to plan such an evening session.

More Information

In this section, you will find further information for publishing possibilities. Look in school equipment catalogs for current prices. If you wish to purchase machines, the following rough estimates of costs will give you an idea of how to budget.

Laminator	$1800.00 (film is sometimes included with machine)
Binder	$1200.00
(500) plastic binders	$89.00 (district discount price)
Service contracts	$281.00 per yr. for laminator★
	$97.00 per yr. for binder

★A service contract for the laminator is strongly recommended for the first year.

Binder (800 System)	$1250.00
(100) binding strips	$43.30
Blank books:	
100 small @ $1.00	$100.00
100 large @ $1.50	$150.00
Filmstrip supplies:	
200-foot blank strip	$8.00
8 pens from art supply store	$10.00
Other art supplies:	$50.00
TOTAL:	$4700.30 (without service contracts)

Bookbinding Instructions

Assemble Materials

- sewn signatures (see next two pages)
- fabric, wallpaper, foil paper, and so on for cover
- glue that won't bleed through fabric or paper
- chipboard (available through teachers' supply catalogues)
- mini Logos
- ruler
- scissors

Directions

1. Measure dimensions of signature to be bound.

2. Cut the cover material approximately 1/2" longer and wider than signature; if using fabric, iron it flat.

3. Cut the chipboard the same size as the signature and then cut the chipboard in half.

4. Center the two pieces of chipboard on the fabric, leaving about 1/4" in the center between them; glue in place.

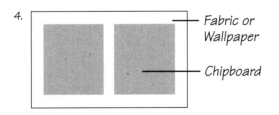

4. — Fabric or Wallpaper — Chipboard

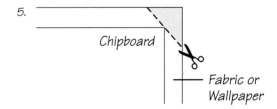

5. Chipboard — Fabric or Wallpaper

5. Cut each of the four corners of the fabric or wallpaper diagonally, close to the corner of the chipboard.

6. Fold the edges of the fabric over the chipboard and glue down.

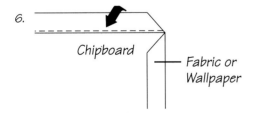

6. Chipboard — Fabric or Wallpaper

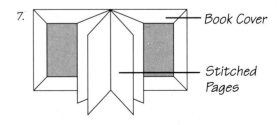

7. — Book Cover — Stitched Pages

7. Open the book cover so that the book lies flat; center the signature inside; glue first and last signature pages onto chipboard.

For further book bindery ideas, see: *How to Make Books with Children* by Joy Evans and Jo Ellen Moore (Teacher Resource Book, Level 1–6), Carmel, California, 1985.

Signature pages are copied back to back. Several pages are then sewn together along the dotted line.

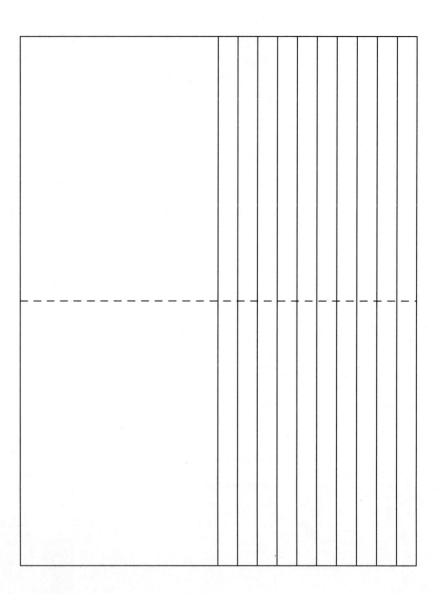

Signature pages are copied back to back. The pages are then separated into two signatures by cutting along the solid center line. Several pages are then sewn together along the dotted line.

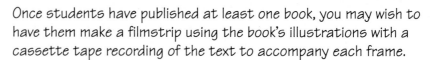

Directions for Creating Sound Filmstrips

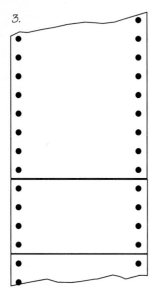

Once students have published at least one book, you may wish to have them make a filmstrip using the book's illustrations with a cassette tape recording of the text to accompany each frame.

Begin by sending a letter home to parents asking them to send a blank cassette tape to school for their child. (See Sample Letter, page 136.)

To produce the sound filmstrip you will need a roll of blank filmstrip, a set of fine-tip permanent markers in various colors, and a blank audio cassette tape. They may be ordered from an audiovisual equipment company.

1. Cut a 14-inch length of blank filmstrip, which will allow for 16 frames.

2. Tape the blank filmstrip to a clean surface.

3. Count eight holes down from the top edge and draw a line between the 8th and 9th holes, using a black fine-tip permanent marker.

4. Count down four more holes and draw the next line. Continue until you have created the number of frames desired.

5. Have students draw illustrations from their published book in each frame, using fine-tip permanent markers.

Note: Always have students draw on the inside of the filmstrip, the side that naturally curls up to form the inner side.

6. Once the illustrated frames are complete, have students record the text that accompanies each frame, using the book they have published as a guide. After the words for each frame have been spoken, use a bell, xylophone, buzzer, triangle, or similar sound to signal the next frame. For example:

"Once there was a sad ghost."

[Sound indicating next frame]

Sample Filmstrip
Sample Filmstrip
Instruction filmstrip: *Making Children's Filmstrips*
When making a filmstrip
measure off 4 holes on film.
Draw a line in the middle.
The film has to be fed into the
projector with the outside facing forward.
This means you have to write on the inside.
(When the film is rolled up it will show which is
inside and which is outside.)
To get correct feed into the projector,
leave two frames blank.

"He lived under a tree."

7. Place the completed filmstrip, cassette tape, and original book in a plastic bag holder in a special section of the Authors' Corner for all to enjoy.

Dear Families,

Because your children have become such enthusiastic authors and illustrators, I have planned to introduce some activities next week that are designed to further encourage their efforts. The activities I have planned include taping their already published stories, making filmstrips based on stories, creating puppets based on characters, turning stories into plays, and making activity sheets (crossword puzzles, riddles, and so on) based on stories.

We will need some supplies in order to begin our projects. If you have any of the items listed below, please send them to school as soon as possible:

shoe boxes

buttons

scraps of felt

scraps of yarn

odd socks

shirt cardboard

blank audio cassettes★

★If your child wishes to tape his or her story and you do not have a blank cassette available, I can purchase one at a discount. The cost of the tape is _____.

Thank you for your continued help!

Sincerely,

Editor's Checklist

Name _____ Date _____

Title of Story _____

Story Problem _____

How Problem is Solved _____

_____

_____

❏ I have used a capital at the beginning of each sentence.

❏ I have used a period (.), question mark (?), or exclamation mark (!) at the end of each sentence.

❏ I have put a circle around any word I am not sure how to spell.

❏ I have used the correct spelling rule for words with suffixes.

❏ I have used quotation marks to show dialogue.

Partner's Signature _____

Place this checklist in your Publishing Pocket along with your Publishing Stick.

WRITING AWARD

THIS IS TO CERTIFY THAT

_____

IS A PUBLISHED AUTHOR

_____
TEACHER

Whole-Language Bibliography

Atwell, Nancie. *In the Middle: Writing, Reading, and Learning with Adolescents.* Portsmouth, N.H.: Heinemann Educational Books, 1987.

Butler, Andrea, and Jan Turbill. *Towards a Reading-Writing Classroom.* Portsmouth, N.H.: Heinemann Educational Books, 1987.

Calkins, Lucy McCormick. *The Art of Teaching Writing.* Portsmouth, N.H.; Heinemann Educational Books, 1983.

————. *Lessons From a Child.* Portsmouth, N.H.: Heinemann Educational Books, 1986.

Cambourne, Brian, and Jan Turbill. *Coping with Chaos.* Portsmouth, N.H.: Heinemann Educational Books, 1987.

Clay, Marie M. *The Early Detection of Reading Difficulties* (3rd edition). Portsmouth, N.H.: Heinemann Educational Books, 1987.

Cochrane, Orin, Donna Cochrane, Sharen Scalena, and Ethel Buchanan. *Reading, Sharing, and Caring* (3rd printing). Winnipeg, Manitoba, Canada: Whole Language Consultants Ltd., 1989.

Cullinan, Bernice E., editor. *Children's Literature in the Reading Program.* Newark, Del.: IRA, 1987.

Goodman, Kenneth. *What's Whole in Whole Language?* Portsmouth, N.H.: Heinemann Educational Books, 1986.

Goodman, Yetta, and Carolyn Burke. *Reading Strategies: Focus on Comprehension.* New York: Holt, Rinehart and Winston, 1980.

Goodman, K., E.B. Smith, R. Merideth, and Y. Goodman. *Language and Thinking in School: A Whole Language Curriculum* (3rd edition). New York: Richard C. Owen Publishers, 1987.

Graves, Donald. *Writing: Teachers and Children at Work.* Portsmouth, N.H.: Heinemann Educational Books, 1983.

Hancoch, Joelie, and Susan Hill, editors. *Literature-Based Reading Programs at Work.* Portsmouth, N.H.: Heinemann Educational Books, 1987.

Hansen, Jane, Thomas Newkirk, and Donald Graves, editors. *Breaking Ground: Relate Reading and Writing in the Elementary School.* Portsmouth, N.H.: Heinemann Educational Books, 1985.

Hansen, Jane. *When Writers Read.* Portsmouth, N.H.: Heinemann Educational Books, 1987.

Holdaway, Donald. *Foundations of Literacy.* New York: Ashton Scholastic, 1979.

Johnson, Terry D., and Daphne R. Louis. *Literacy Through Literature.* Portsmouth, N.H.: Heinemann Educational Books, 1987.

McVitty, Walter, editor. *Getting it Together: Organizing the Reading-Writing Classroom.* Primary English Teaching Association (PETA), Portsmouth, N.H., Heinemann Educational Books, 1986.

Newkirk, Thomas, and Nancie Atwell, editors. *Understanding Writing—Ways of Observing, Learning and Teaching K-8.* Portsmouth, N.H.: Heinemann Educational Books, 1986.

Newman, Judith. *Whole Language: Theory in Use.* Portsmouth, N.H.: Heinemann Educational Books, 1985.

Norton, Donna. *Through the Eyes of a Child: An Introduction to Children's Literature* (2nd edition). Columbus, Ohio: Charles F. Merrill, 1987.

Turbill, Jan, editor. *No Better Way to Teach Writing!* Primary English Teacfhing Association (PETA), Portsmouth, N.H.: Heinemann Educational Books, 1982.